PASSIONS

JOHANN SEBASTIAN BACH:

A STAGE PLAY

karen klami

PASSIONS
JOHANN SEBASTIAN BACH: A STAGE PLAY
Copyright © 2022 by karen klami
ISBN: 978-1-60571-620-6
All rights reserved

ShiresPress
Manchester Center, VT 05255

Printed in the United States of America

Handmaidens (mixed media/acrylic on canvas, 65" x 45")

Rita Fuchsberg
Artist

**Cover art & all details from *The Visitor*
(acrylic on canvas, 16" x 20")**

My art is spontaneous and mixed media/acrylic on canvas is my preferred medium. The pieces begin with two flat layers of white gesso and a third layer applied as one would ice a cake. The surface, when dry, has valleys and uneven plains and forms the foundation from which the work will take on a life of its own and accidents are part of the process.

A piece can appear to represent one image and then flip into another. The interpretation is in the eye of the beholder. My heritage informs my imagery. I paint because of an inner necessity to do so.

Several of my works have been exhibited throughout the United States and are part of collections in Africa, Australia and France.

My time is divided between a studio in what my mother calls "a one-horse town" in Vermont, and my hometown, New York City. I live with my shih-tzu, Coco.

rdiane1950@hotmail.com

dedicated

to

my beloved husband

Leslie Klami

who is my very own Sebastian

and so much more

PASSIONS

a play in two acts

by

Karen Klami

© 2022

Passions – Karen Klami

Passions – Karen Klami

CHARACTERS:

Johann Sebastian Bach (age 36-65)
Anna Magdalena Bach (age 20-49) – Second wife
Wilhelm Friedemann Bach (age 11 to adult) – Son from first marriage
Carl Philipp Emmanuel Bach (age 8 to adult) – Son from first marriage

3 Male Actors playing the following roles:
Man 1 (various)
Man 2 (various)
Prince Leopold of Anhalt-Cöthen
Priest
Dr. Born, Member of Leipzig Council
Dr. Deyling, Superintendent of St. Thomas
Voices of Leipzig Council
Lorenz Mizler (Mitzler), student and philosopher
Johann Ludwig Krebs, student
Gottfried Theodor Krause (good student)
Johann Gottlieb Krause (bad student)
Johann Adolph Scheibe, critic and writer
Frederick the Great (II of Prussia)
Officer in Frederick's court
Old Musician Jonas in Frederick's court
Doctor Chevalier John Taylor, eye surgeon

2 Women Actors playing the following roles:
Woman 1 (various)
Woman 2 (various)
Friederike Henriette, wife of Prince Leopold
Woman of the French Court of Leopold
Mrs. Wolff, Church Council Member, Leipzig
Angelina Wolff, daughter of Mrs. Wolff

SETTING AND TIME:

Act 1:
Bach Home , Leipzig, 1750 and Cöthen, 1721-22
Court of Prince Leopold of Anhalt-Cöthen
Churches

Act 2:
Bach Home in Leipzig, 1722-1750
St. Thomas School, Church, Choir Loft and Office, Leipzig

Passions – Karen Klami

ACT 1 SCENE 1

Before Rise: JS Bach music plays before lights are up. Varied, selected and very upbeat pieces. Ends with the blast from the Kyrie of the B Minor Mass, which fades as the lights come up to silence.

At Rise: All is in silence. The room is dark, but for light coming in from a window, late afternoon sun in March, Leipzig, 1750. It is the kitchen or common room of a humble dwelling. There is a large table with comfortable chairs. To one side there is a wood stove and other kitchen paraphernalia. There is a harpsichord in the room

> (Sound of outside horse drawn carriage coming to a stop. Voices, a man and a woman's, indistinct words which sound close to "Easy. Slowly. Alright, then. Thank you." Door opens to let in more afternoon light. ANNA, age 49, looking much younger, enters, leaving the door open behind her and quickly moves to light a lamp, which she brings back to the doorway. She waits rather impatiently, then returns into the room to pull a chair from the table and place it far from the table. There is a rustling outside the door, to which she responds by running back to the door, and in her haste, nearly falling over the chair she has just moved. She holds the lamp up high at the door, then steps back, allowing SEBASTIAN, age 65, to enter. His eyes and face are bandaged so that he cannot see at all. SEBASTIAN walks forward as if he were able to see clearly and is about to crash into the chair which ANNA has moved out. She gets to the chair before him, and puts out her hands to stop him. He meets them full-stride, then stops abruptly.

SEBASTIAN
What?

ANNA
I...
> (trying to direct him to move back by touching him)

SEBASTIAN
> (pushing her hands away and putting out his hands toward her in a stopping motion)

Don't!
> (ANNA unhappily steps aside. SEBASTIAN steps forward slowly, feeling out in front to feel the chair)

Why? I told you....

ANNA
I know.

(ANNA stands off to the side, helplessly watching as SEBASTIAN takes chair and pushes it miraculously into its proper place at the table. He then finds his way around the table, not without some difficulty to which ANNA makes a motion toward him, thinks better of it and stops. HE has found a particular chair, pulls it out and sits. This was quite an effort, and SEBASTIAN sits, looking rather exhausted. ANNA watches a moment, in silence, then starts to remove her outer garments, hanging them on a hook. ANNA moves to SEBASTIAN to remove his outer clothing. He hears her coming toward him and puts out his hand to stop her. She stands still, then retreats, and he lowers his hand.)

SEBASTIAN
Not now!
    (quietly)
Thank you, Anna. Not…now.
    (silence)
Why is it so quiet? I'm not going deaf, too, am I?

ANNA
The quiet was intended.

SEBASTIAN
This? No, this is a stifling silence. I can hear my own heart pounding.

ANNA
It's hard for them to see you like this.

SEBASTIAN
Hard for *them*?
    (Silence)
Is he…?

ANNA
Tomorrow.

SEBASTIAN
Is he so preoccupied with his fancy life he has no time for me?

ANNA
Tomorrow. You need to rest today.

SEBASTIAN
Rest.
(Laughs)
All I've done for a week is wait and rest and rest and wait some more and for what? More useless sloth for the blind man?

> (He stands and begins to remove his outer garments. ANNA watches at a distance. She is feeling quite helpless as he struggles with the coat. He removes it, turns and starts to walk toward where he would hang it. He starts out cautiously, then walks full stride into the end of a cabinet near the spot, where he stops, almost falling from the blow, and feeling disoriented, he holds onto the cabinet for balance as ANNA rushes to him and helps him back to the chair.)

ANNA
You stubborn fool! If you want to emasculate yourself on a piece of furniture, do you think you can wait until after I'm gone?

SEBASTIAN
(Still in pain, but laughing)
What?

ANNA
There are parts of you that I love, and then there are parts of you that I *love*. Let's not lose *all* those parts in one day.
> (He shows signs of being in pain in the area of his eyes. She helps him back to the chair. She pulls over a chair and sits beside him and strokes his head)

Bad?

SEBASTIAN
Much worse. Worse than the first time. The stabs are deeper inside my head. I believe the surgeon's dug out more forkfuls of my brain and has been pulling them through my eye sockets.

ANNA
I hear there are universities who offer large sums for brain matter and eyes. I will be sure to contact one.

SEBASTIAN
Mine are old. Much too old. And tired. Weak. And ugly and…

> (ANNA puts her hand on his lips to shush him. She strokes his cheek, then his lips again. She takes his head in both her hands and gently kisses him. He touches her face, examining each part of it by touch. She is moved, and again kisses him. They kiss more passionately. He moves his hands down her neck to stroke her breast, basically taking each one in hand. She stops him, pulling away, but gently and not far.)

ANNA
Ah! So all parts are intact and working after all.

SEBASTIAN
Coffee.

ANNA
What?

SEBASTIAN
Coffee. A mug of coffee before I turn into a goat.

ANNA
That you already are.

SEBASTIAN
Nectar of the gods. This god needs his nectar.

ANNA
Yes. All gods of the house are present and accounted for.

SEBASTIAN
> (Rises and starts toward the clavichord. He follows the edge of furniture to arrive there.)
Except one prominent demi-god.

ANNA
Friede would beg to differ with you on that. He…
> (ANNA, busy with the coffee, only catches a glimpse of what he is doing near the end of it. But SEBASTIAN has seated himself and starts to play the first Kyrie from the B Minor Mass. This is the first piece of music we have heard in the play. ANNA stops everything and listens)

ANNA (Cont'd)
I know it. Is it the Kyrie?
> (SEBASTIAN keeps playing and doesn't answer. ANNA starts to hum it, and then she sings)

"Kyrie, Eleison…Eleison…Eleison…"
> (Upon hearing ANNA sing, SEBASTIAN stops playing)

SEBASTIAN
You still sound extraordinary. Even more beautiful than when I first heard you. That sound. Wondrous sonic beam. I looked all over the room. Where could that amazing and enchanting sound be coming from? And there it was. Anna Magdalena Wülken. The court's own darling. Smug and so proud of herself.

ANNA
Some things will never change…cannot change….
> (Each scene will flow into the next. ANNA will rise and go to SEBASTIAN and remove his bandages as he continues to play music on the harpsichord.)

ACT 1 SCENE 2

(Early summer, 1721, Zerbst. From the scene before, SEBASTIAN is playing the clavichord in 1750, as ANNA unwraps the bandages from SEBASIAN'S eyes. The scene changes around them to a church christening. SEBASTIAN stops playing, as imperceptibly, music of BUXTEHUDE begins to be played on an organ very quietly. (Dietrich Buxtehude at the Schnitger Organ in Norden, Ulrik Spang-Hanssen, organ. 1. Chorale Prelude "Christ, unser Herr, zum Jordan kam" BuxWV 180, 2. Chorale Prelude "Erhalt uns Herr, bei deinem Wort" BuxWV 185) ANNA is now being dressed in a veil, as for church, and something which suggests her youth. SEBASTIAN'S clothing has also been changed to suggest a younger man. As he is being changed, A PRIEST enters dressed in robes, followed by a MAN and a WOMAN carrying an infant to a baptismal font. ANNA has moved to one side and is now offstage. Music changes to Telemann Aria "Jesu, komm in meiner Seele," and ANNA begins to sing. (Teresa Stich-Randall unearthly beautiful Telemann aria, G.F.TELEMANN Cantata "Machet die Tore weit", Aria:"Jesu, komm in meiner Seele". – Jesus, come into my soul. Kurt Equiluz, tenor; Ernst Schramm, bass; Teresa Stich-Randall, sop; Nedda Casei alt; Vienna State Opera O & C; Wilfried Bottcher Concert hall SMS 2486.) SEBASTIAN'S eyes follow up to where she seems to be, unseen to audience, but not to him. He is transfixed, smiling, moved. She sings angelically, as the baby's Baptism takes place with the PRIEST speaking prayers in Latin, MAN and WOMAN holding the baby over the font, water being poured over its head, as the baby cries. MAN, WOMAN and PRIEST walk off as ANNA ends the song. She has descended from above. We have watched SEBASTIAN'S eyes follow her down. When she is level, he turns and almost hides. ANNA enters, sees him, and looks as if she would speak, but doesn't, continuing to go past him. SEBASTIAN turns in time to see her from behind, quickly follows after her, as he calls out)

SEBASTIAN

Anna Magdalena Wülcken?
(ANNA hesitates and turns)

SEBASTIAN (Cont'd)
Of the Wülcken trumpeters? Johann Caspar Wülcken. And son-in-law. And sons of sons-in-laws. All trumpeters?

ANNA
I've never heard it put that way, but yes. I am of the Wülcken Trumpeters.

SEBASTIAN
I'm...

ANNA
I know very well who you are.

SEBASTIAN
I doubt it.

ANNA
What?

SEBASTIAN
That you know me.

ANNA
Rather you mean that I would want to know you?

SEBASTIAN
What I mean is that you may have heard of my music, and that I am the Kepellmeister at Arnhalt-Cöthen for Prince Leopold and his very French Court. But that is hardly knowing me.

ANNA
I should say that *was* knowing you very well.

SEBASTIAN
Then who am I?

ANNA
Pious. Deep. Sometimes tortured.

SEBASTIAN
Tortured?

ANNA
Yes. At least that is my interpretation. It is what I heard in one of your arias. Awful!

SEBASTIAN
Awful?

ANNA
"Dearest God, Have mercy on me, Grant me solace and grace. My sins afflict me, Like *pus* in my bones, Help me, Jesus, Lamb of God, I am *sinking* in *mire*."
    (pause)
I sang it. At court. You are all the rage, Johann Sebastian Bach. "Painfully spiritually poetic," I think one of them said. Some were very moved by your work. Though others seemed to favor Handel's compositions. They said he was a "light hearted genius" over your "heavy handed morose view of the sinful state of man." That's a rough translation of the French.

SEBASTIAN
And I was thinking I could impress you with my knowledge of *your* family's fame. You astound me. It is as if I already know you very well.

ANNA
Are we somehow related, that you say you know me well?

SEBASTIAN
We're back to that again. Well, who really *knows* another human being? Only God.

ANNA
I wonder.

SEBASTIAN
Yes. As a matter of fact, we have...I have...already met you, in a way.
    (pause, looking her over, making ANNA a little uncomfortable)
But, you were fatter then.

ANNA
What?

SEBASTIAN
Chubby, I'd say. Round about the middle. Like those puffed up little cherubs the Italians paint. You were, oh, I'd say, eight.

ANNA
Eight? Eight years old? Where?

SEBASTIAN
Halle. It was a competition for the organist's post. But that isn't where I saw you. It was later. At the Church of Our Lady. A christening.

ANNA
I was at least ten when I was at Halle.

SEBASTIAN
Twelve, actually. You were accompanied by, of all things, three trumpets, all playing very loudly, but in a low, dark register. Your voice rang up, and out, and through it all, like a great, strong, radiant beam of light.

ANNA
I do remember that. But I was never round as a little Italian cherub!

SEBASTIAN
Big Italian cherub. No. Of course not. But you sang like one. An angel, straight from the throne of God. Just like now. Like a dream, but alive, before me. Flesh and bone, to touch.
    (pause, staring at her, then in a whisper)
Beautiful beyond measure.

ANNA
Thank you.
    (pause, as she stares back. She is smitten. Then coming out
    of it)
But I wasn't round.

SEBASTIAN
An enormous, plump Italian cherub.

ANNA
An angel. You said an *angel*.

SEBATIAN
So I did.
    (long pause as they look at one another)

ANNA
    (turning away)
Did you get the organist's post?

SEBASTIAN
No. No, I didn't.

ANNA
Pity.

SEBASTIAN
Yes.

ANNA
Shameful, really. With your talents, ambition...

SEBASTIAN
It wasn't God's will.

ANNA
God's...? *God's* will? Now you sound like my father.

SEBASTIAN
I'm too old fashioned for even my own generation. But, look. Will you let me...
    (moves to ANNA)
I'd like to...

ANNA
Yes?

SEBASTIAN
I would....would you...?
    (moves closer to ANNA)

ANNA
(affirming)
Yes.
(noise from off as WOMAN 1 comes to fetch ANNA)

WOMAN 1
Good! There you are! We're leaving for the reception.

ANNA
Actually, I've invited Herr Bach to accompany me.

WOMAN 1
That wasn't necessary. He's already been invited. He's part of the family.

ANNA
Really?

SEBASTIAN
I'm one of the godparents.

ANNA
So am I. A godparent.

SEBASTIAN
So we are related after all. Bloodlines through spiritual means.

ANNA
Yes. Spiritual.

SEBASTIAN
Shall we.
(offers ANNA his arm and she takes it. They begin to walk off, arm in arm. MAN 2 and WOMAN 2 enter, stop and then look at them, whispering to one another. WOMAN 1 joins them)

ANNA
We're causing quite a stir.
(SEBASTIAN takes this as his cue to let go of her arm, but ANNA holds onto him tightly)
No. No, stay. I rather like the attention.

SEBASTIAN
(letting go, but gently)
I don't.
(MAN 1 enters and approaches SEBASTIAN upon seeing him)

MAN 1
Herr Bach.
(turning to ANNA, with a short nod of the head)
Anna. Your singing was lovely.
(before she can answer, back to SEBASTIAN)
I'm so pleased you are still here.

SEBASTIAN
I'm sorry if I kept you waiting. But I was communing with the angels and couldn't tear myself away.
(winks at ANNA, who smiles, but turns away)

MAN 1
I understand you completely. That I do. But, if I may be so bold, we were wondering if you would play for us one of your own compositions at the reception? Maybe something you created for his Excellency, Prince Leopold? Or one of your concertos for the Margrave of Brandenburg, perhaps? Whatever suits you, my friend. We would be so grateful....

(SEBASTIAN and MAN 2 exit, followed by WOMAN 1, WOMAN 2, and MAN 2. ANNA, having been left behind, ignored, shakes her head at this. She then does a comical flapping of wings with her arms)

ANNA
Fat, indeed!

(She smiles, as she leaves, as if flying after them. As ANNA exits, scene is changing into the next, with SEBASTIAN playing a clavichord or harpsichord offstage. ANNA enters soon, dressed in her 1750 attire. ANNA remains onstage as SEBASTIAN is offstage, playing.)

(Back in 1750. We hear a real choir singing and orchestra of: Bach - B minor Mass - 25 - Dona nobis pacem - Karl Richter, ANNA enters in her older attire carrying the Calov Bible Commentary which SEBASTIAN has annotated, and the other is an original manuscript written by ANNA of her poetry. As she enters, the "Dona nobis pacem" subsides and is taken over by SEBASTIAN, remains offstage, playing on a clavichord or harpsichord. He plays parts of The Art of the Fugue, Contrapunctus 4 & 13, the Goldberg Variations, the B Minor Mass Crucifixus, etc. Pieces to use:
Contrapuntus 1, 4, 11 & 13, WTC Prelude in C;
Art of fugue - Contrapunctus 4 – Gould,
Art of fugue - Contrapunctus 13 – Gould,
Goldberg Variations for keyboard – Gould, Goldberg Variations (Part 1 of 6),
B Minor Mass, Need a keyboard performance of: XIII. Mass in B minor ~ Crucifixus
Goldberg Variations var.26-30 & Aria Da Capo – Gould,
SEBASTIAN is playing WTC Prelude in C Minor

ANNA
Sebastian? Sebastian! I won't read to you while you play.
(He stops playing while she is in mid-sentence, so she shouts the next phrase)
I'm not going to shout...
(Stops, sighs, smiles, now quoting the Bible, part of Deuteronomy 32:2)
"...my speech shall distil as the dew, as the small rain upon the tender herb, and as the showers upon the grass."
(Silence)
Sebastian? Can you hear me?
(SEBASTIAN resumes playing: WTC Prelude in C. She shouts over it)
Oh, stop it! You don't know it, do you? You can't stand it when I can quote a scripture passage that you don't know!

SEBASTIAN
(Stops playing, calling from offstage)
Okay. It is somewhere in the Old Testament.

ANNA
That certainly narrows it down.

SEBASTIAN
Not the Psalms. Maybe Proverbs...

ANNA
Give up?

SEBASTIAN
Never!
 (SEBASTIAN plays as ANNA speaks above it)

ANNA
Be as stubborn as you like, but you will never get it. It's in the book of Deuteronomy, chapter 32 and verse 2. Ha! There! It has taken most of my life, but I now can quote scripture passages as well as you. A lot good that has done me.
 (Pulls out a letter which was inside the Calov Bible commentary, and while SEBASTIAN now plays: Contrapunctus 4. She is shouting)
Sebastian. Here's another morsel for you. "His music would be the admiration of whole nations if you didn't take away the natural elements in your pieces by giving them a turgid and confused style, and if you didn't darken their beauty by an excess of art."
 (He stops playing abruptly. Silence)
I thought that might get your attention.

SEBASTIAN
That isn't God's word.

ANNA
No. These are from a demi-god. Herr Johann Adolph Scheibe, to be precise.

SEBASTIAN
Anna?

ANNA
Yes, almighty one.

SEBASTIAN
Don't blaspheme.
 (SEBASTIAN plays: Contrapunctus 13)

ANNA

Herr Scheibe is the one blaspheming. "Self-importance has led him from the natural to the artificial, and from the lofty to the somber. One admires the onerous labor and uncommon effort, which, however, are vainly employed, since they conflict with Nature."
> (At this SEBASTIAN stops playing. Silence. Then he begins to play: Mass in B minor ~ Crucifixus.)

On the other hand....
> (Putting down the letter, and paging through the Calov)

This you have marked, so vigorously with many underlines..."David used his psaltery to please God, and to kindle his heart towards God...but *they* misuse if for entertainment, to satisfy their own ears."
> (pause)

When the council begs you to simplify, you make your music more complicated, "To please God." And this, to satisfy *you*, the only one who knows what music pleases God.
> (SEBASTIAN begins to play again: Goldberg Variations var.26-30 & Aria Da. ANNA opens Calov and reads)

Here's a gem. You've underlined the whole passage. Matthew chapter 6, verse 25. "Therefore, I tell you, do not be concerned about your life, what you shall eat or what you shall drink, nor about your body, what you shall put on."
> (Laughs ironically)

"Do not be concerned about your life..." Our life. All our lives entwined into this big mess of a....oh what does it matter?
> (SEBASTIAN stops playing. Silence a moment, then he begins to play WTC 1 C Major. ANNA picks up her poetry book collection, pages through, stops at one page)

Do you remember this? I wonder. It's about you, my love. *YOU.*
> (She stands, reading a poem from the book, "I Sit and Watch."
> SEBASTIAN stops playing to listen)

"I sit and watch, undulating massive hands moving to and fro.
great falcons, birds of prey.
what comes of it?
sounds and stars, both lighting up the universe.
my universe.
inside and out.
revealed to me in greater measure by my tears as I listen, rapt and dancing together.
my heart and mind entwined in joy.
ecstatic breath.

                        ANNA (Cont'd)
a rhythm in light and shadow into dreams and back.
wearing an earthly body to disguise this piece of art, all mine, so great.
a heavenly thought embodied in a man."
> (as ANNA finishes, and pauses, as if in deep thought, then speaks)

My beloved…my darling…I…

> (SEBASTIAN immediately interrupts her with music. But this is different. This is a blast from an organ, which, of course, is not in the house. It is SEBASTIAN playing the Toccata and Fugue in D Minor for the next scene)

ACT 1 SCENE 4

>(1721. ANNA does a simple change from older to young ANNA attire. SEBASTIAN, unseen, is playing the Toccata & Fugue in D Minor, but in fits and starts. He is changing the organ's register, then blasting it. ANNA listens and gets lost in the music, enchanted. When he plays some big and heavy spots, she imitates him in a comic way, then smiles and stops. The music has stopped, but ANNA is still doing some of this imitating with no music, enjoying her exaggerations. Young SEBASTIAN enters with a manuscript. He smiles at ANNA, looking first puzzled, then amused)

SEBASTIAN
You have my technique down very well, but I thought I lifted my right hand a little higher.
>(ANNA wheels round, embarrassed)

Oh, don't stop. It's like looking into a distorted mirror. You recognize yourself, but you hope you don't really look that bad.

ANNA
I was entertaining myself while I waited.

SEBASTIAN
Waited?
>(taking the time to say each part of her name as he walks around her)

Anna, why are you here? To sing? Some occasion?

ANNA
No. I was told the organ was having her "lungs tested." Was I mad to come?

SEBASTIAN
To listen to such a long and tedious task? Yes, you were. But I'm glad you did.
>(SEBASTIAN takes her hand, kisses it, does a bow, quotes *Song of Solomon*)

"My dove, my perfect one...Fair as the moon, Clear as the sun..."

ANNA
Hmm?

SEBASTIAN
Sing for me.

ANNA
What? No. Here? Why?

SEBASTIAN
Won't you sing for me?

ANNA
(indicating herself)
Do you want to test these lungs as you do the organ's? To see if they satisfy?
(pause)
Do they?
(pause)
Satisfy?

SEBASTIAN
Ever since I heard you at the christening. It is the most perfect sound I have ever encountered among God's creation. The birds grow silent to listen to you.

ANNA
That is too much, really.

SEBASTIAN
God knows what is too much and what is the truth. I am telling the truth.

ANNA
What was that last piece you played? Is it your own?

SEBASTIAN
Yes. The D minor toccata and fugue. It has everything one needs to hear if she, the organ, can sing in any register in full voice. I pull out all the stops and play in the fullest possible texture, in order to see if the organ has "good lungs."

ANNA
She sounded glorious. Do you ever use vocal music?

SEBASTIAN
No.

ANNA
I think your vocal melodies soar, yet they're rooted somehow, fitting perfectly into the human voice. I know. I've sung some which are quite difficult, and yet, I find myself floating note to note, effortlessly. Still, the music is virtuosic. How do you do it?

SEBASTIAN
Soaring music, like birds, is something only God creates. I just listen and put it down. *I'm* listening, but I'm not sure anyone else is. Likely, when I am gone, all this...
    (indicating manuscript)
...will become the paper used to wrap fish for sale or make silly hats for children.
    (pause)
Music for virtuosos, huh? More often I have been accused of writing unwieldy and tedious exercises for children's fingers to master.

ANNA
There's that word again. Tedious. Is that how you feel about what you do? Your life?

SEBASTIAN
My life is an open book. Before men, anyway. But God's eyes reach farther in and see what's hidden in the heart. Before Him I am entirely naked. What can I hide from Him?

ANNA
Actually, to tell the truth, I have been...investigating you, since we last met. Looking into your reputation a little more closely. Beyond how you are viewed at court.

SEBASTIAN
And?

ANNA
Disappointing.

SEBASTIAN
Really? Why? What have you uncovered? Please. Enlighten me.

ANNA
Well, first of all, that you are a deeply religious man.

SEBASTIAN
Religious? In a fashion, yes.

ANNA
In character, some say you are harsh. Devouring students, choirs, and musicians all at once, like a dragon.

SEBASTIAN
Old news.

ANNA
Others say distant. Stiff, perhaps. Aloof.

SEBASTIAN
Nothing startling there.

ANNA
And that you will, if provoked, have fits of quoting vast passages of scripture by heart.

SEBASTIAN
I confess, I have done that, yes.

ANNA
Then I imagine I will be given the pleasure of listening to your "fits of scripture" from time to time?

SEBASTIAN
No doubt. If provoked. And you...you have provoked me! By your very presence. It overwhelms me, like being hit by a large stone right to the forehead.

ANNA
Don't be silly.

SEBASTIAN

Like David hitting Goliath. Whop! Powerful and quick. It is about to overtake me.
> (acting as if he can't control himself)

My God in heaven! It is upon me!

ANNA
> (looks amused, then a little startled)

This is most amusing....I think...

SEBASTIAN

I cannot contain it! I must pronounce it now!
> (as if preparing to speak in a very loud voice, ANNA cringes. He then speaks quietly, almost in a whisper, and quotes from the Bible, *Song of Solomon*)

"Let him kiss me with the kisses of his mouth! For your love is better than wine...Draw me after you; let us run. The king has brought me into his chambers."
> (stops)

And so it goes on for chapters. Her song of him. Her love. How he satisfies her.

ANNA

I...

SEBASTIAN

And his response is...well...he sings...
> (quoting again, he moves around ANNA, as if examining her)

"Your lips are like a scarlet thread, and your mouth is lovely. Your cheeks are like halves of a pomegranate behind your veil. Your neck is like the tower of David, built in rows of stone; on it hang a thousand shields, all of them shields of warriors. Your two breasts are like two fawns, twins of a gazelle, that graze among the lilies. You are altogether beautiful, my love; there is no flaw in you."
> (SEBASTIAN stops, watching ANNA'S expression)

ANNA

Quite a performance. And that was....?

SEBASTIAN

Song of Solomon.

ANNA
That?

SEBASTIAN
Yes, *that*. Holy Scripture. Apparently God isn't vague or shy about extolling one of the extreme joys of mankind. Shall I continue? I know quite a lot more.

ANNA
No! No, you've made your point. I see I may like to have scripture quoted to me quite a lot in our days together. That's if you don't mind?

SEBASTIAN
That was my plan.

ANNA
Yours? And what about God's plan?

SEBASTIAN
He knows my heart.

ANNA
Yes. But does He know mine?

SEBASTIAN
I do.
(SEBASTIAN moves toward ANNA, and they kiss in a quiet and gentle, but passionate way. As they part, MAN enters abruptly, not really paying mind to what has just happened. They are both startled)

MAN
Herr Bach? There you are. Well, what do you think of our organ? Can you give us a good report? Does she sing? Does she *satisfy*?

(SEBASTIAN and ANNA look at one another and laugh. MAN laughs, but doesn't know why. SEBASTIAN takes the MAN by the arm and leads him off while speaking)

SEBASTIAN
Yes, she sings beautifully in the top registers and holds her own. I am wondering about the lower registers....

> (ANNA remains on stage. The next scene is being set up for ANNA to go back to 1750, as older ANNA. She puts on her older attire, and sits at a table, which has her poetry book lying open on it)

ACT 1 SCENE 5

>(1750. ANNA, alone, reads aloud from her poetry book. FRIEDE enters, unseen)

ANNA
"your fragrance arrived in the room, miles before your words. I floated on it as one does in a memory of complete rapture and innocence. you pulled in my heart with your gossamer string smile, glittering and wet with possibilities and the taste of dreams. whatever you actually said was blanketed in streams of morning and evening and rainbow, obscured with grand and luminous preoccupation of joy. gently, softly, a whisper blew inside me and took that which sparked long before my own time could remember and was rekindled. it leapt into your arms, waiting, trusting they would hold and not falter. under the weight of so glorious a day as this, when you kissed the stars within me back, alive again."

FRIEDE
I still don't know why Father never used you as a lyricist. Your words are transporting…and true. He has never appreciated that part of your talents.

ANNA
>(at first surprised, then relieved, going to him for an embrace)

Friede!

>(FRIEDE holding ANNA long, so she almost pulls away. FRIEDE goes to the book of ANNA'S poems, which he picks up and pages through. ANNA seems a little uneasy)

FRIEDE
Ah, Angelica!

ANNA
And my Ruggiero.

FRIEDE
This has really grown. Many more than I remember. All as passionate as the ones I read?

ANNA
Nothing has changed, Friede. Nothing.

FRIEDE
Everything's changed. When my mother died, when you came, when I went.

ANNA
Good changes.

FRIEDE
More like a life of little fugues. Fast and furious. One line following frantically upon another. Twisted changes. Inversions. Nothing is the same. It never can be right again. Never.
    (Smiles, changing the subject to Sebastian's state, nodding
      toward offstage)
So?

ANNA
We won't know for quite some time.

FRIEDE
Is he...?

ANNA
Barely. His strength isn't what it was. Then again...

FRIEDE
Then again.
    (They both laugh)
Was this...?

ANNA
Much worse than the first time. He knew what to expect. Those torture instruments. And the pain. It is a horrible operation, and I...I...

FRIEDE
It was his decision. No one could ever turn his mind around. Rest. We can do nothing more than wait. Again.

ANNA
He was asking for you. Angry you weren't at the door to greet him when he got home.

FRIEDE
Was he? What about Carl? I'm sure he asked for him.

ANNA
No. He asked for you.

FRIEDE
What does he want from me, damn it?

ANNA
Oh, Friede, what has he always wanted?

FRIEDE
No. That won't...no.

ANNA
You torture yourself for no good reason.

FRIEDE
Don't stoop to lies and tell me about how much he loves me, okay?

ANNA
I wasn't going to.

FRIEDE
I always got that all wrong, anyway.

ANNA
What?

FRIEDE
(Long pause, looking at ANNA)
Love.

ANNA
You were a child.

FRIEDE
I knew my own mind. And better yet, *he* knew my mind.

ANNA
That's...it's all so far in the past, Friede. Distant, like a dream.

FRIEDE

Is it?

    (Moves to ANNA and touches her face)

It springs to life every moment I see you. It has never really died. You are still as lovely as the first day he brought you home. Like one of those porcelain dolls, with no flaw. Perfect. I never saw anything more enchanting. God, what a day that was. I was so full of rage and passion, all fighting inside me for the same space. All ten years of my little life. I was ten, wasn't I? Eleven? I can't remember now. How did I survive?

    (FRIEDE exits, at first lingering his hand on ANNA'S face, then moving off quickly. ANNA stays put, changing back into her young ANNA attire. The scene changes.)

ACT 1 SCENE 6

> (Cöthen, November, 1721. ANNA remains on stage as we hear SEBASTIAN'S voice off stage, bellowing out FRIEDE'S name)

SEBASTIAN
Wilhelm Friedemann Bach!
> (young SEBASTIAN enters, moving to ANNA)

ANNA
Are you sure I should meet them here, today. It seems so soon.

SEBASTIAN
Soon? We'll be married in a month and you call this soon?

ANNA
Maybe if I met them outside the home. There are so many memories of their mother here.

SEBASTIAN
They will have to get over it.

ANNA
How can they get over the death of their mother. They are still very young, and you don't just...

SEBASTIAN
They are nearly men. And age means nothing. I had to get over it. Death. So do they.
(FRIEDE enters. He is now 11 years old and acts like a young boy)
Here we are. This is Willy. Wilhelm Friedemann. Where is Carl? Willy is the oldest. How old are you now?

FRIEDE
Eleven. They're still at lessons.

SEBASTIAN
> (To ANNA)

Ah, yes. Latin.

ANNA
Oh.

FRIEDE
(To SEBASTIAN, while eying ANNA)
Is this her?

SEBASTIAN
Yes. This is Anna Magdalena Wülcken.

FRIEDE
You can't be my mother. You're too young.

ANNA
No....not your mother. No.

FRIEDE
You look like a portrait of someone. You're quite beautiful. There's a painting by Cecco Bravo. You look like a goddess he painted.

ANNA
Really?

FRIEDE
Angelica. It is Angelica and Ruggiero. He saves her from the Orca. Then he jumps off his flying horse to get his reward from her, which is a thousand kisses. But she uses her magic ring to disappear. It's a myth.

ANNA
I wish it wasn't. A thousand kisses sounds like a very appealing reward.

FRIEDE
Italian painters are not like the German ones. Italians paint real emotions. Germans paint stiff people gaping and staring.

SEBASTIAN
Angelica and Ruggiero. It is quite charming, you know. He especially likes those Italian painters who are fond of bare breasts.
(ANNA looks at SEBASTIAN)
They hang in full view for, well, just anyone...especially Germans...to "gape and stare" at, in public, passed off as art. The Catholic Church has been supporting these artists for years. These Artists of the Naked. They get a lot of viewings for it.

FRIEDE
They're beautiful.

SEBASTIAN
I will admit, they are. But they are a little *too* much so to you.

ANNA
If he...well, he's just a boy, but...

SEBASTIAN
If he's attracted to them that much? Then I'd say he's a *man*.

FRIEDE
I know you appreciate true beauty and these painters paint true beauty.

SEBASTIAN
(Moving to ANNA and embracing her)
This is true beauty. This is painted on my heart, Willy. And I don't have to show it off, naked, to the world.

FRIEDE
No, Father. You are too full of sacred thoughts to ever want to show off mere fleshly pleasures.
(SEBASTIAN looks hard at FRIEDE)

ANNA
(Lightly)
I'd say he's a man, yes. And a very clever one. They call you Willy, but I'm going to call you Friede. Friedemann is a better fit for you than Wilhelm. Friedemann means Man of Peace. Wilhelm means a Man of War. Conqueror. One who is always wearing his helmet.
(Touches FRIEDE's head; he pulls away)
But you don't need a helmet to hide that enchanted mind of yours. Strange that you should be named for both a man of war and a man of peace.

SEBASTIAN
That isn't surprising to me. He has an obviously strong head, but exceptional talent. He has already shown great ability in improvisation on the harpsichord. *And* in composition. Outside of that, he's, well, he's always been a bit confused.

FRIEDE
No, I'm not!

ANNA
He doesn't look confused at all. Angry, maybe. But not confused.

FRIEDE
I'm not angry or confused or anything you have to say about me. You're wrong.

ANNA
Not about your being Friede.

FRIEDE
You have no right to name me. My mother named me and I won't have you change it. You're not beautiful like the goddess at all. You're...you're ugly!

SEBASTIAN
Willy!

ANNA
No. Friede. His name is Friede and I won't have you call him anything else. He's full of truth and wisdom, this Friede, and I want him to be called by his proper name from now on.

FRIEDE
Why? Why should I let you?

ANNA
(Eyes on FRIEDE)
Because you and I both know it is true. You *are* a man of peace. I can see it in your eyes.

FRIEDE
(Looks at her a long time, studying her up and down)
I was wrong. You are Angelica.
(Pause, still looking studying her)
But only...only if I can be Ruggiero.

ANNA
Yes, of course...Friede.

                         FRIEDE
    (Smiles)
Alright...alright then...
    (Goes to ANNA, takes her hand, bows and kisses it)
Come with me.

    (FRIEDE holds ANNA'S hand as he is leading her off. ANNA
    looks back at SEBASTIAN as if to say "I told you so."
    SEBASTIAN smiles, unconvinced, sighs, looks as if he would say
    something, then stops, and follows them out. Set changes to a
    church, with no one on stage.)

ACT 1 SCENE 7

(December 3, 1721 - Wedding of Anna and Sebastian. Set is transformed into a church setting, but it actually took place at a chapel at at Leopold's Court. The music is on organ, Bach's Air on a G String.

Air on the G String (from Suite No. 3 in D; arr. Virgil Fox)

ANNA and SEBASTIAN enter, with ANNA wearing a veil and white robe representing her wedding dress, and SEBASTIAN in some kind of robe representing his wedding garment. A PRIEST in robes is marring them as they kneel before him. FRIEDE, CPE and two other WOMEN, enter and are seated as if in the church. As the PRIEST is apparently speaking and having SEBASTIAN and ANNA respond with the vows, but we can't hear anything because of the music, FRIEDE watches uncomfortably. CPE is watching him (we don't know it is CPE yet) but then becomes occupied, as if praying in church. ANNA and SEBASTIAN aren't aware of FRIEDE'S being uncomfortable. ANNA and SEBSASTIAN are at the part of the ceremony where they kiss, and FRIEDE rises, agitated. The PRIEST blesses them and leaves.

ANNA turns to FRIEDE and offers with her hand extended for him to join her and SEBASTIAN up at the altar, but FRIEDE storms off. ANNA and SEBASTIAN are joined by the two WOMEN and CPE, who congratulate them. ANNA and SEBASTIAN then walk off that spot and move to another, as ANNA is helped out of her wedding veil and robe, and SEBASTIAN out of his "wedding robe," as the set is changed for the Court of Prince Leopold for the next scene. We hear the sound of ANNA singing with SEBASTIAN playing a clavichord. It is "Bist du bei mir")

Bach~Bist du bei mir – Ingrid Kertisi

Bist du bei mir, G. H. Stölzel / J. S. Bach (BWV 508), from Notebook for Anna Magdalena Bach

ACT 1 SCENE 8

>(December 5, 1721. At the Court of Leopold of Anhalt-Cothen. LEOPOLD is seated with his Viola da Gamba, listening to SEBASTIAN playing and ANNA singing. The WOMEN who have helped ANNA change leave and will return later in the scene, one as FRIEDERIKE and the other as a WOMAN OF THE COURT. ANNA and SEBASTIAN finish the song to exuberant applause from LEOPOLD, as he stands.)

>LEOPOLD

Astounding. Really. Anna, you cannot have brought that to a higher place. What a talent in your little package. What a wife, Herr Bach.

>ANNA

I am pleased to have pleased you...as pleasing is a pleasure doubled in your presence.

>LEOPOLD

Poetry abounds today! Thank you Anna Magdalena Bach, new bride of my very pleasing Kapellmeister. And you....that melody....you are extraordinary.

>SEBASTIAN

It's not mine. The melody belongs to Gottfried Heinrich Stolzel.

>LEOPOLD

And the arrangement?

>SEBASTIAN

Mine.

>LEOPOLD

Can you put in a part for me? I'm itching for a new piece to play the viola da gamba.

>SEBASTIAN

After the wedding.

LEOPOLD
Yes. Weddings. One upon the other. And here you are, so soon after yours entertaining me. And mine in less than a week. I would like that sung at our reception. Will you, Anna?

ANNA
Of course.

SEBASTIAN
Will it....*please* the princess....duchess...?

LEOPOLD
My new wife? No. Nothing will please her except my arms around her. Or so she claims. But I am wasting time. I want you to come with me to see if you can fix the pedal harpsichord. It sticks.

SEBASTIAN
Where?

LEOPOLD
Everywhere. It will be just a moment.

ANNA
Of course.

(ANNA curtseys as LEOPOLD and SEBASTIAN exit. ANNA is alone, as FRIEDERIKE enters with a WOMAN OF THE COURT. They are speaking in French. They see ANNA, acknowledge her with a nod, but continue in French. ANNA acts as if she doesn't understand them, but she does. Every word.)

FRIEDERIKE
Je suis consterné par la façon dont mon adore Léopold que l'homme. Il adore lui.

WOMAN
Pardonne. My French. It is weak.

FRIEDERIKE
(Speaking quietly to the side, as if to hide what she is saying from ANNA)

I am appalled at how my Leopold adores that man. He dotes on him. He is too generous. And that old music he composes. Leopold struggles to play it. Alors indigne.
(WOMAN looks confused. She speaks softly, annoyed)
So undignified.

WOMAN
Oui. I have seen it. Et sa nouvelle épouse? (And his new wife?)
(THEY eye her, acting as if they aren't, but ANNA knows she has been eyed)

FRIEDERIKE
Alors...très jeune et jolie
(WOMAN looks confused, speaks emphatically)
So very young and pretty to be married to him. He's so....énorme...huge....et les vieux. And old. Triste, vraiment. (sad, really) So sad.

WOMAN
Les hommes de...les hommes des... Large men are said to be larger...plus grand...much larger than life in bed.

FRIEDERIKE
Ah! Alors qui est l'attraction! So that *is* the attraction! I should have known. Regardez-la. Pauvre petite. (Look at her. Poor little thing.) He'll be dead long before her and she will have wasted her youth and bloom on him.

(BOTH WOMAN laugh. Again, catching the eye of ANNA, nodding acknowledgment to her, THEY exit. LEOPOLD returns)

LEOPOLD
I'm afraid it will be a little more work than I thought. The pedals are really off. I played on them too roughly the other evening. I killed them.

ANNA
I am glad you enjoyed them to death.

LEOPOLD
You are such a delight, Anna. What a surprise he would find you after Maria Barbara. So many tragedies, yet here you are, like the blessed sunshine after a storm.

ANNA
I am the one who is blessed.

LEOPOLD
I wonder. You know, your husband was just now making a mockery of my talents.

ANNA
Why am I not surprised?

LEOPOLD
He won't let me play my fiddle on his little fugue until I have mastered some of the others. Why not? I can do it. That one in G minor...what a joy. It is a big gift in a little package. I want to play all of it. Maybe he will play it and I will dance to it.

ANNA
Dancing to a fugue?

LEOPOLD
Yes, I know. But I enjoy it. Your husband has inspired me so. I feel much like David. He danced before God and was exhilarated. I imagine his dances were primitive. Intoxicating. Stirring emotions. Not like this age of refinement and etiquette. I'd rather dance as David did.

ANNA
His wife didn't share his enthusiasm. Nor does yours. I saw the Princess just now, and she spoke of my husband's influences on you in...enlightening terms.

LEOPOLD
What did she say?

ANNA
I have to translate it from the French.

LEOPOLD
She spoke in French?

ANNA
Yes.

LEOPOLD
And you understood?

ANNA
Yes.

LEOPOLD
Did she know you understood?

ANNA
No.

LEOPOLD
You'll have to excuse her....how can I put it? Her lack of musical appreciation. She is a modern woman, adopting the fashion of the day.

ANNA
She is ...amusa.

LEOPOLD
She has neither ear nor desire to enjoy any music. I am sorry. When she speaks French...

ANNA
She is very *frank*....ish.

LEOPOLD
Frankish? Very good. When she speaks in...*frankish*...she often speaks about things she doesn't really understand. I am sorry. But you see...I am in love with her. Madly.

ANNA
I understand.

LEOPOLD

Thank you.
    (There is a moment of between them. SEBASTIAN returns. To
    SEBASTIAN)
Hopeless?

SEBASTIAN

Fixed and as good as new. I intend to play that harpsichord at your wedding.

LEOPOLD

Then I will play, too. At my wedding *and* at my birthday. We will all play that G minor fugue. I won't take no for an answer.

SEBASTIAN

Alright, we'll practice it. And I'll write more dance suites for you, with challenging parts. Then you can play and sing to your heart's content.

LEOPOLD

Like the old days. Come, now. Let's practice my birthday cantata.

SEBASTIAN

Right now?

LEOPOLD

(Grabbing his viola da gamba and a chair)
And I will play my fiddle.

    (SEBASTIAN sits at the harpsichord, ANNA stands next to him,
    and LEOPOLD places the chair so that he has his back to the
    audience, and plays the viola da gamba as they play the
    minuet: J. S. Bach - Cantata "Durchlauchtster Leopold" BWV
    173a (2/2). As they play, the scene changes)

ACT 1 SCENE 9

(Cöthen, Bach home, 1722. The scene changes to the Bach home. ANNA exits with LEOPOLD, as SEBASTIAN changes to playing the Minuet in G Major, BWV 841 from Anna's Notebook of 1722, **not** the one in the 1725 Notebook. Later in the scene he will play the C Minor Prelude from Anna's 1725 Notebook. and Minuet in G Major, the Minuet in G Major BWV Anh.114 by Christian Petzold (THIS is the one from the 1725 Notebook). FRIEDE will play from his Notebook, BWV 927, Prelude in F major; BWV 928, Prelude in F major; and BWV 930, Prelude in G minor.
CPE and FRIEDE enter, pulling in a second harpsichord on wheels, and plant it next to the one at which SEBASTIAN is playing. They act exuberant and like young boys of 11 and 9. As SEBASTIAN continues to play, FRIEDE does an exaggerated imitation of court dancing. SEBASTIAN seems to not mind and plays on)

FRIEDE
(Doing a dance move to every part of CPE's name)
Dance with me, Carl...Philipp....Emmanuel.....Bach..... Like the Prince and his wife.

CPE
His wife doesn't like to dance and neither do I.
(SEBASTIAN ends it. FRIEDE does an exaggerated bow. CPE laughs and applauds.)

SEBASTIAN
Is that applause for the player or the French Court's dancer?

FRIEDE
Both. Father and son. That was from the practice book for Anna, wasn't it?

SEBASTIAN
Yes. What do you think of it?

FRIEDE
It's...alright.

SEBASTIAN

Just *alright?*

FRIEDE

(Fingering the manuscript of the Notebook)
There's not much in her book yet, is there? Mine is full. But I'll bet there is nothing in there that compares to this one of my own...
> (FRIEDE sits down at the other harpsichord and starts to play the Prelude in F Major BWV 927 from his Notebook. He plays fast and furious, shows off his virtuosic talents.)

CPE

Oh, that's my favorite one from *your* book, Friede. Can I play it with you?

FRIEDE

(While playing)
Go ahead....if you can keep up!
> (CPE sits and plays very well, but can't keep up. FRIEDE stops and laughs, stands, and does his exaggerated bow again, and CPE once more applauds him)

SEBASTIAN

That was...*alright.*
> (FRIEDE is visibly annoyed, but SEBASTIAN smiles and they both laugh.)

FRIEDE

I compose **and** play well enough to get your goat, don't I?

SEBASTIAN

What about this?
> (SEBASTIAN sits at the harpsichord and plays the C Minor Prelude which will be in Anna's Notebook of 1725. FRIEDE starts to do an exaggerated dance making funny faces as he does and tries to pull up CPE to dance with him.)

CPE

Not now. I want to listen.
> (FRIEDE stops, sits and listens. He seems to be moved in spite of himself. SEBASTIAN pays it to the end. There is silence while he plays, then a long pause)

SEBASTIAN
What's the matter?

FRIEDE
It is heavenly. Written for...an angel.

SEBASTIAN
You never cease to surprise me, Friede.

CPE
He's the clever one.

SEBASTIAN
No, Carl. You're the clever one. He's the moody one.

FRIEDE
I am not! I am a level headed fellow, as long as you don't cross me. Then I have the temper of a dragon. Just like you. And I know exactly what you would say after a long and hard day's work of hours and hours of composing and copying out?

SEBASTIAN
And what is that?

FRIEDE
A round of ale for all!
    (ANNA enters with an arm full of copy paper, quill pens, ink bottles and a rastrum for drawing staff lines all at one time.)

ANNA
What are you talking about ale?

FRIEDE
A round of ale for all! And a good smoking pipe to go with it!
    (Sits up on the table, raising an imaginary stein and pipe)
To the Bach family protégés.

SEBASTIAN
    (Raising an imaginary stein)
To God who gives such gifts to mere men.
    (THEY clink their imaginary steins together)

ANNA
Bunch of clowns. Harlequins.

CPE
A Harlequin?

ANNA
In the theatre he is a wise servant who pretends to be a fool.

CPE
Oh. I heard someone call father that.
  (FRIEDE gives CPE a look)

SEBASTIAN
Really? Who?

CPE
The organ builder. Herr Scheibe.

FRIEDE
No. Herr Scheibe's *son*, Johann Adolph Scheibe, the lesser. He said you played the fool for the Court, while you hide your ambitions up your sleeves. That's when he called you that.

SEBASTIAN
He means a *musikant*.

FRIEDE
What's that?

SEBASTIAN
A strolling player. Minstrel. Fool in the court of the Prince. At fourteen years old he has quite a shipload of opinions. His father is a strong man. I am not surprised the son is as well.

ANNA
  (Laying out the manuscript paper and pens and ink on the table)
Isn't it about time we started copying out the Passion passages? Friede, sit here. Carl, next to him.

(ANNA lays out manuscript paper, pens and ink. Gives CPE the rastrum)

SEBASTIAN
His manuscript is too poor.

ANNA
It has improved greatly, hasn't it, Carl? And he is very good at making the staff with the rastrum. He has a steady hand and doesn't smear it.

CPE
And I can read all the music I copy out.

SEBASTIAN
Very well. But you will have to waste time proofreading their work.

ANNA
I don't mind.
(SEBASTIAN pulls out manuscript, divides it into sections, speaking almost to himself)

SEBASTIAN
Young men with criticisms of things they don't understand. "Free thinkers," they are calling themselves, yet they are trapped into whatever they hear that comes from a far and distant land, and thinking it is exotic, eat it up.

ANNA
Don't trouble yourself.

FRIEDE
I'd rather not copy out now.
(getting up from the table and going to the harpsichord)
I'd rather play. Or compose myself.

ANNA
You know it is hard to copy out one thing when listening to another.

SEBASTIAN
Let him play. Let him play this.
(Taking out a piece of music from elsewhere)

FRIEDE
I'd rather play my own preludes.

SEBASTIAN
Then I can assume you are not **able** to play this because it is not familiar to you.

FRIEDE
You know that isn't true. My sight reading is superior to anyone's, even you.

SEBSTIAN
Then prove it by playing this. And if you make a mistake, even a little one, you will have to stop completely, and I win.

FRIEDE
I accept the challenge.

SEBASTIAN
Good. Here.
    (FRIEDE takes the piece of music and is about to look at it)
No peeking! Just put it up there. I will count to three, and then you must play it flawlessly.

ANNA
Why do you pressure him?

FRIEDE
I don't feel pressure. This is exciting.
(puts music on harpsichord, looking away, and seats himself and gets ready)

SEBASTIAN
Alright then. One…two…three….

> (FRIEDE looks up and after just a mere second's hesitation, he begins to play the Minuet in G from Anna's 1725 Notebook. He plays beautifully, flawlessly and seems to be moved as he plays, to tears. ALL listen attentively and are moved as well. When he finishes, there is long pause. He is unable to speak. CPE stands, applauds.)

CPE

Friede is the winner!
> (FRIEDE doesn't rise, but still sits, deeply moved. He picks up the music and holds it)

FRIEDE

This is one of the most beautiful things I have ever heard. My fingers danced when I played it. They couldn't help it.

SEBASTIAN

And the playing was perfect. Thank you. I am very pleased.
> (Going to ANNA and putting his arms around her. FREIDE seems disturbed)

You. That is for Anna's new book. The melody isn't mine, alas. It is by Christian Petzol. I...
> (FRIEDE throws the music to the ground.)

FRIEDE

You never wrote anything like this for *my* mother!

SEBASTIAN

Friede! Stop it!

ANNA

Let him be.

SEBASTIAN

He is out of control!

> (FRIEDE plays BWV 928, Prelude in F major, and BWV 930, Prelude in G minor. He goes from one to the other, playing them fast and furiously, even though they are not fast pieces. FRIEDE's playing drowns out SEBSASTIAN's and ANNA's words)

FRIEDE

You frolicked and danced and drank your ale and left us here to rot. You write this for her and my mother rots in her grave.

ANNA

Friede, you have to stop it.

FRIEDE

(Stops playing)

How could you marry him? He's like David. Except instead of killing a man, he killed his wife to marry you, Bathsheba. You married a murderer.

(SEBASTIAN lets out a roaring sound, which frightens everyone. He turns, calmly speaking)

SEBASTIAN

Oh, God in heaven. Forgive me.

(He walks out of the room. FRIEDE is stunned. ALL are silent. FRIEDE quietly picks up the music he has thrown, carefully puts it together, handing it to ANNA. FRIEDE exits. ANNA stands, stunned and still. CPE remains seated at the table. Suddenly the sound of the eighteen piece Capella of Leopold's is heard. They are playing the Brandenburg Concerto No. 6 in B Flat Major, BWV 101, 1st movement. The Viola Da Gamba part is conspicuously loud. You can hear the harpsichord, too, very well. Scene changes immediately to Leopold's Court. As ANNA and CPE exit, and there is the change of set, LEOPOLD will enter with SEBASTIAN from off, as if just coming from having played with the Capella.)

ACT 1 SCENE 10

(Fall, 1722. At Leopold's Court. Suddenly the sound of the eighteen piece Capella of Leopold's is heard. They are playing the Brandenburg Concerto No. 6 in B Flat Major, BWV 101, 1st movement. The Viola Da Gamba part is conspicuously loud. LEOPOLD enters with SEBASTIAN from off, as if just from having played with the Capella, to join ANNA, WOMAN and MAN of the court)

LEOPOLD
That was truly magnificent. You must write in more parts for me in those concertos.
    (Seeing ANNA and MAN and WOMAN, to them)
La musique. Manifique.
    (They nod in agreement)
Friederike wants me to learn to speak more French, for the court, but I'm not very good.

ANNA
No, that was excellent. I have also been teaching it to Kapellmeister Bach, my Prince.

LEOPOLD
Really? Let's hear it. It will be good for me. I'll step back and listen.

SEBASTIAN
I am also very new at it.

ANNA
Then this is a good time for practice. Here, with Madame and Monsieur.
    (calling them to her)
Voulez-vous venir un moment, s'il vous plaît.? Kapellmeister voudrais vous parler.
    (to SEBASTIAN)
Talk to them.

SEBASTIAN
No...I. Bonjour. Comment va tu?

WOMAN
Bonjour, Kapellmesiter. Tres bien. Tres bien.

SEBASTIAN

I...um...Je...Je voudrais savoir....
> (looks at ANNA, who approves and cheers him on)

Je...J'aime avoir un message du ***cul.***
> (WOMAN and MAN look shocked, then laugh)

Madame Anna donne de bons messages du...

ANNA

Cou! Cou.

SEBASTIAN

Oui. Hier, j'ai entendu...une Francais...une...***faire le con***, avec une grande interest.
> (WOMEN covers her face. MAN smiles with appreciation. ANNA closes her eyes, is about to speak, but doesn't. LEOPOLD laughs aloud, then stifles it)

MAN

Je suis certain que c'était très gratifiant.

WOMAN

> (still covering her mouth)

Oui, oui! Très gratifiant!

SEBASTIAN

Je désire acheter un cadeau pour ma femme pour d'anniversaire. Quel est la...***foutu*** cadeau en France?

MAN

Vous l'avez déjà dit. Faire le con de son mari. Très approprié est cadeau.

WOMAN

Idiot!
> (hits the man playfully, but is very embarrassed, LEOPOLD smiles)

ANNA

Merci, mes amis. Vous avez été très... utile.

WOMAN
Très amusant!
    (THEY exit. SEBASTIAN looks puzzled. ANNA looks at LEOPOLD)

LEOPOLD
I sense it was not nearly the success you had anticipated, Madame Bach.

ANNA
No.

LEOPOLD
I understood only a fraction, but what I did…well…
    (turns to SEBASTIAN, with a grin)
You cursed up a storm.

SEBASTIAN
I cursed?

LEOPOLD
You asked if a proper gift for a wife on their anniversary was his…um…
    (indicates body part, then starts to laugh)

SEBASTIAN
I have never used that kind of language in my life.

ANNA
Oh, but you've wanted to.

LEOPOLD
We will both need to practice our français, my dear friend. But for now, I must leave you. Friederike is planning a gala march of my footmen around the city on my birthday. She loves parades and soldiers. Well, then, until tomorrow, Kapellmeister. Anna.

SEBASTIAN
Yes, my Prince.
    (ANNA curtseys, SEBASTIAN bows, LEOPOLD exits. To ANNA a little agitated)
So what *did* I say?

ANNA
You said you'd heard a...well, an *intimate moment* with great interest. And your enjoyment of my messages was not of the neck, but of the *derriere*.

SEBASTIAN
Why didn't you stop me? They said idiot. I understood that. I was an idiot to try.

ANNA
Hardly. You made a valiant effort.

SEBASTIAN
I was a fool. They have no patience for someone like me.

ANNA
Like you? There is no one in the universe like you.

SEBASTIAN
Thank God, Almighty.

ANNA
I do. Je t'aime, mon bel homme.

SEBASTIAN
No more French, please.

ANNA
No. No, my love.

(SEBASTIAN exits, as lights go down. Scene changes to Bach home, with ANNA, putting on an apron. She is now at the table, making pastries)

ACT 1 SCENE 11

> (1722. In the house at Cöthen. ANNA is at the table, which is covered with all her ingredient for making a flakey French pastry and sugar-cream filling. FRIEDE enters, and sits down. ANNA says nothing)

FRIEDE
What are you making?

ANNA
You shouldn't be here. You shouldn't be in here at all. You should still be at your lessons. Why are you home?

FRIEDE
What does it matter? So, what are you making? Tell me or I will tickle it out of you.
> (FRIEDE gets up and starts to tickle ANNA)

ANNA
Okay, okay, okay! I'm making you a new kind of dessert... a pastry... French... for a celebration for your...
> (FRIEDE, while tickling her, tries to grab some sugar-cream from the bowl. ANNA is swatting FRIEDE away from bowl)

....for you getting such high honors in Latin! Get away!

FRIEDE
With creamy sugar inside?
> (puts his finger into the bowl, takes some and licks it, then takes more on his finger and offers it to ANNA, she refuses)

ANNA
You're making a mess.

FRIEDE
Things like this are always messy.
> (offers it to her again. She still refuses. He touches her lips with his finger with the cream on it and gets some on her)

ANNA
Friede! Stop it. I don't want it.
> (licking it with her tongue and wiping it with her hand.)

FRIEDE
But it is all so *sweet*!
> (FRIEDE swings round and does it again. He has one arm around her and with the hand with the cream, he touches her face)

ANNA
You fiend! Stop it!
> (ANNA is laughing. FRIEDE stares into ANNA's eyes. She looks at him questioningly, then smiles)

FRIEDE
So sweet.
> (He embraces her and kisses her deeply on the mouth)

There. Now you know.
> (ANNA steps back a little stunned)

ANNA
Yes, I guess I do....know....something...but I'm not sure I truly understand.

FRIEDE
Didn't you suspect?

ANNA
I...no...what?

FRIEDE
Oh, now don't be hurt about it. After all this is rather...like...Adam and Eve. In the garden. Innocent.

ANNA
I wouldn't go so far as to call it innocent, exactly.

FRIEDE
Don't you feel it too?

ANNA
Feel what? Friede, calm down. I don't know what....

                           FRIEDE
Don't be shy. You can say it. You're...we're...it's the garden of
paradise...

                            ANNA
This place? I don't think so, no. I wish it was. Your father...

                           FRIEDE
My father? Aren't father's meant to benefit their sons? Raise their
station above their own out of love? How has he ever benefitted me?
Does he really have such a perfect plan for my life when he crushes my
every dream and desire?

                            ANNA
What dreams and desires?

                           FRIEDE
There are no possibilities! Everything is dead. I will be what he wants,
not what I want.

                            ANNA
What do you want?

                           FRIEDE
Passion. You have no idea what real passion is. How can you? You
married a man who could be *your* father, too. What about you, Anna
Magdalena Wülcken? What do you ache for in your bed at night? Does
the body lying beside you provide what you need or do you pine away
for more?

                            ANNA
Your father is more a man than anyone, young or old, could ever be. I
won't answer you except to say that your father loves you deeply and
wants to help you with...

                           FRIEDE
I don't need his kind of help. What I want to help myself to is here,
right before me. Can't you see it? I say *you* pine...but, really, *I*
pine...for *you*.
         (FRIEDE approaches ANNA, but she moves back)

ANNA
Friede....Friede, you're jealous of him.
> (FRIEDE stops)

I saw your anger at your father and your need for a mother when I came here. I just thought when you witnessed her death, it was too much. I just thought you were sad...and frightened. But you're jealous.

FRIEDE
I'm not jealous. Of him? How can I be? But you. You could never be my mother.

ANNA
No, I am not your mother.

FRIEDE
> (moving to ANNA)

I want you. I have wanted you the moment I called you Angelica.

ANNA
This is no good.
> (FRIEDE embraces her and begins to kiss her on the neck. He puts his head on her chest, and embraces her. She lets him and there is a moment between them, but then FRIEDE takes her head in his hands and kisses her on the mouth. ANNA pulls away)

FRIEDE
You *do* want me. I can feel it.

ANNA
No. No. I don't. What you feel is my deep sorrow for you. That is all.

FRIEDE
Alright, then. Go breed like a rabbit with him! If that is all you desire, then that is all you are fit for.

> (FRIEDE leaves. ANNA stands, stunned, then recovers, and continues to methodically make the pastry. She stops, then breaks down and cries, sitting down. A bowl falls to the floor, smashing into pieces. Change to next scene starts. ANNA takes out her book of poetry and begins to read "Glorious Day")

ANNA

glorious day, and I will sing for you more gloriously than glorious can. and I will weep more bitterly than bitterly can weep, if you but move one inch from me. where can I go that will be as radiantly lit as looking into your eyes, and see suns upon suns
with kissing galaxies? where is the place that reaches farther into me than your words and looks? I embark and ride into strange hands in peril of my very being when I breath in your breath of love. glorious day, and I will sing all the more of loving you.
    (pause)
you are a fountain to me. the more I drink from you, the more I want.
    (pause)
Oh, Sebastian...

    (ANNA picks up her book, and some of the pieces of the broken bowl, and then exits with them in hand.)

ACT 1 SCENE 12

> (November, 1722. Leopold's Court. LEOPOLD is playing the harpsichord, practicing the WTC Book 1 E Minor Prelude. SEBASTIAN is listening offstage and speaks from there)

SEBASTIAN
You aren't using all your fingers, my Prince. I am hearing too many thumbs.

LEOPOLD
How can you tell what fingers I'm using from all the way over there?

SEBASTIAN
I wrote it. I should know the best fingering for it. And I don't believe you began your practice with a prayer.

LEOPOLD
What prayer?

SEBEASTIAN
The one at the top of the page.

LEOPOLD
Where?
> (SEBASTIAN enters carrying a satchel with the Leopold's birthday cantata. He goes directly to LEOPOLD and points to the top of the page he is playing, and he reads it)

"I.N.J, In Nonime Jesu." I prefer the J.J. version, "Jesu, help me!" Much more my attitude as I try to play your music. And I didn't pray it. No wonder I am all thumbs. Better leave this for another time. I have something I need to talk to you about.

SEBASTIAN
If it is about your birthday cantata, I have busy as a bee with it. Here.
> (SEBASTIAN hands him a manuscript from the satchel. LEOPOLD reads it to himself, then aloud)

LEOPOLD
"Golden sunlight's happy hours, Those which very heaven gathers, Make again now their appearance; Praising, singing, tune the lyres, That his fame may be extended!

LEOPOLD (Cont'd)
Thy name shall like the sun go forth, E're whiling midst the stars shall stand!
Leopold in Anhalt's borders, Shall in princely fame be glorious. "You make much of me, like a heavenly angel or demi-god, and not a mere prince of this world.

SEBASTIAN
You are a worthy despot to be praised for the good you have done. Let me play this.
> (SEBASTIAN sits at the harpsichord and plays a part of that section: It is the Cantata BWV 173a Durchlauchster Leopold, Birthday of Prince Leopold of Anhalt-Cöthen. LEOPOLD continues to look at the manuscript and notices something on it)

LEOPOLD
What is this at the top? A seal? Is it a Bach family seal? What a masterpiece. Who designed it?
> (SEBASTIAN stops playing)

SEBASTIAN
I did.
> (goes to LEOPOLD and shows him each part of it)

There are the twin monograms of my initials, facing one another, like a mirror, with this in the middle, a mediator between them. It is all very symmetrical. Like the universe.

LEOPOLD
Why the crown on top of the mediator?

SEBASTIAN
I won't say. My little secret. Let someone try to discern its meaning.

LEOPOLD
Then it has special meaning?

SEBASTIAN
You will have to trust me that if anyone decides to examine it in detail, they will not be disappointed.

LEOPOLD
(hands page back to SEBASTIAN)
Trust you. Yes, trusting someone can be a sticky predicament, can't it?

SEBASTIAN
Who can we really trust but God?

LEOPOLD
Trust Anna. You are lucky to have such a wife. She's your salvation. Your heart.

SEBASTIAN
She is my heart, yes, but not my salvation.

LEOPOLD
You are too pious, my friend. Too removed from the present, in your own little world of the past starry skies, when the world seemed magical and happy. Magic is being sucked out and replaced with a cold and harsh thorny truth.
(pause, softly)
Amusa.

SEBASTIAN
What?

LEOPOLD
Amusa. Without a muse. No inspiration. No music inside. That is my Friedericke.

SEBASTIAN
You're quite the poet today.

LEOPOLD
Each morning, as I arise from my bed, and I look back at what has kept me warm and satisfied in the night, I see a goddess, now transformed into a mere human, feeble, female. Yet...*yet* there is still nectar in it. And in my gut is an insatiable desire for it.
(pauses, thinking deeply. SEBASTIAN seems smitten, but confused)
So...Friederike is not happy with the delicacies you produce. They are too complicated for her. She wants marching armies with marching bands. Bravado and spectacle.

LEOPOLD (Cont'd)
(leans in close to SEBASTIAN, as if pleading)
I need to please her. I can't help myself. I am in love. Smitten with no hope. You must understand.
(more formal, as SEBASTIAN is reacting without speaking, in anger)
I will write you a glowing letter to whomever you wish to apply. I will hold nothing back. And you will remain Kapellmeister here, forever. That is your title and you will keep it. But as for my court...if I don't end it quickly, it will die a slow, choking death. You see?

SEBASTIAN
You spoke of trust? What kind of trust did you mean? The kind that is betrayed? I won't believe it. We were like brothers!

LEOPOLD
I am your *Prince*, Kapellmeister! I am your *authority* and I have made my decision. Yes, we are like brothers. But I have to do this. Can't you see it? What would you do for Anna? Tell me? What mountains would you not level for her?

SEBASTIAN
Any but this.
(gets satchel and moves to exit)
Anna was right. You should have remained alone.
(bows low)
My Prince.

(SEBASTIAN exits, leaving LEOPOLD'S cantata behind. LEOPOLD picks it up and looks at it, then sighs with terrific emotional pain. Lights down)

ACT 1 SCENE 13

> (Lights up to reveal SEBASTIAN standing searching around the room, with ANNA sitting on the floor, repairing, with stitching, an old, comfortable chair.
> We are now in Leipzig, July-August, 1723. They have been here since May 22. It is a house which is attached to the Thomas School. The room they are in is the parlor of their living quarters. It is spacious, with windows (four) overlooking Leipzig's city moat and surrounding meadows. There is a harpsichord on wheels, so that it can be moved from place to place. There is a good deal of comfortable furniture, but things are in a general disarray. Mainly musical things are out and about, instruments, music in large piles, and many books, including a Lutheran Bible and The Calov Bible Commentary. ANNA mends the chair watching SEBASTIAN looks for something in piles of music which he can't find. She glances up calmly as she watches him getting more and more irritated)

SEBASTIAN
What are you fixing?

ANNA
My favorite chair.

SEBASTIAN
You mean my favorite chair.

ANNA
Until you fell asleep in it with your pipe and nearly burned the house down.

SEBASTIAN
I said I was sorry about that. It looks so small in this cavern of a room.

ANNA
You mean this decorated cave with the moat outside.

SEBASTIAN
What?

ANNA
What are you looking for, my love?

SEBASTIAN
Everything! Something.

ANNA
Tell me.

SEBASTIAN
The text of the aria from Sunday last. "How they tremble and waver…"

ANNA
"…the thoughts of the sinners." Yes, that happy number. Over here.
    (ANNA retrieves it from a pile near her, barely looking at the pile, and not getting up from where she is, but holding it up for SEBASTIAN to take from her. He takes it from her with a look of surprise. She is has a sly smile.)

SEBASTIAN
And how did you know what I…?

ANNA
I have ears.
    (SEBASTIAN still doesn't understand)
I kept it out. I thought you'd like to have another look at it after I heard what they said about it after the service last week. They bellowed as loudly as they could about how much it moved them to, what did they say? "Pious worship, inspiring them to reverent action." Adding, afterwards, in hushed tones, that having to endure that kind of inspiration Sunday after Sunday was going to be akin a holy call to "crawling on one's bare belly through a thorny hedge." Quite poetic, actually.

SEBASTIAN
Just as bad yesterday, I am afraid. I don't understand what they want.

ANNA
I am surprised. After that whole chain of mediocre musicians?

SEBASTIAN
I wouldn't call them mediocre. They are all seasoned men.

ANNA

They interviewed a flock of woodpeckers disguised as musicians, who played their music as if they were pecking up a winding staircase, and you don't have a clue?

SEBASTIAN

Woodpeckers? I wouldn't call Herr Telemann a woodpecker.

ANNA

What did you call them all, then?

SEBASTIAN

The fatalities.

ANNA

They would have hired any one of them if they said yes. But they had to start as far back in the line as "T", and work their way forward, through many letters, until they settled for landing on "B" for Bach. Or is it "B" for bold? Or bombastic?

SEBASTIAN

At least it's wasn't "B" for boring. However, All those gentlemen who were considered for the post before me are simply deluded in their musical conceptions. For instance, I will show you. A little Herr Telemann here.
  (playing part of Fantasia)
Herr Graupner...there.
  (playing – Three Partitas)
Maybe throw in a pinch of Herr Georg Balthasar Schott.
  (playing – rather light version of above)
Top it off with a wee bit of Herr Rolle.
  (plays a rather dark run of notes, and then continues playing
  more lightly)
And you have it all in a fine dry pudding. The style has been reduced to stock ideas, easily followed and easily taught. Shallow construction of fugal subjects that one hears *ad nausium* in the Italian repertoire. Empty sequences. Lifeless, revealing nothing. No metaphysical ecstasies here.

ANNA

Ecstasies?

SEBASTIAN
(stops playing)
Shallow, like the empty compliments that tickle the ear, but leave one panting like a deer for more substance.

ANNA
Like the council's compliments before the whispering gossip of their true feelings?

SEBASTIAN
(exactly, in French)
Exactement!

ANNA
Ah! French Court talk! I love it when you speak French.
(SEBASTAIN leans down to ANNA, kissing her on the head.)

SEBASTIAN
(pronouncing mare as "MA-rie," which is German for mare)
Mare cheri!

ANNA
I am not a horse! MA cheri! MA! A mare is a female horse! Will you never learn?

SEBASTIAN
(neighing like a horse and shaking his head "no")
Neigh!

ANNA
Very funny.

SEBASTIAN
Nothing is...funny. Nothing about...never mind.

ANNA
I miss it.

SEBASTIAN
What?

ANNA

Cöthen. Leopold has another wife, now. Charlotte Friederike. She loves music and understands the value of a real Kapellmeister.

SEBASTIAN

Please don't.
    (ANNA gets up and goes to a drawer and pulls out a letter.)

ANNA

I copied this out. It was too important to not have our own copy.
    (reading)
"By the Grace of God, We, Leopold, Prince of...
    (SEBASTIAN walks away and busies himself, going through piles of music)
We, Leopold, Prince of Anhalt-Cöthen..." Etc...etc... "...have at all times been well content with his discharge of duties..."
    (looking up, SEBASTIAN says nothing, she continues reading)
"...but, the said Bach, wishing now to seek his fortune elsewhere..."
    (looking up)
What a novel notion. "Seek his fortune elsewhere." Is that why we are here? In these big, empty rooms, in a big, empty city, run by a big, empty-headed council?

SEBASTIAN

Anna. I don't want you to...

ANNA

"...has accordingly most humbly petitioned Us to grant him a most gracious dismissal..." And so on and so forth, with our dear prince's seal affixed thereto.
    (she folds it, lovingly)
What a kindly prince. Worthy to be called a great and fair price among men. And a beautiful letter, really. Releasing us from heaven...into this hell. Why don't you care? Why don't you ever care? They lied about everything.

SEBASIAN

Not about everything.

ANNA

Everything! For the past two months I have heard nothing but excuses for changes and adjustments and belittling you and creating all kinds of problems and indignations.

SEBASTIAN

You know why we left Cöthen. Do you have to make it worse? I miss it, too.

ANNA

I miss being happy.
    (SEBASTIAN moves close to ANNA, and embraces her from the back. She looks as if she would pull away, but doesn't. SEBASTIAN kisses her neck.)

SEBASTIAN

Vexation, envy and persecution follow me. Always.

ANNA

What?

SEBASTIAN

Vexation, envy and persecution. It is a trident spear which I have had to endure. But…can't you see that the boys will benefit from their education, here, at the Thomas School? And I'm composing music for the glory of God in two churches. It's astounding.
    (wooing her with kisses on her neck and arms)

ANNA

For God, yes. But the council lied about your salary. And they lied when they said…

SEBASTIAN

And for you, just beyond these walls, are beautiful parks and promenades where the river flows. And lavish gardens.

ANNA

With thorns and thistles, choking the healthy plants.

SEBASTIAN
And the boulevard inns adorned with frescoes. And coffee houses. Ah! The smell of the coffee houses. Leipzig is like a little Paris at our doorstep. An Elysian fields. And this, here. This house. It will be our Garden of Eden.
>(turns ANNA around)

With you, it already is. Be fruitful and multiply.
>(ANNA looks as if she would protest, but instead smiles. SEBASTIAN kisses her a little more passionately than she expected, then plants his hand on her breast)

ANNA
Like Adam and Eve in the garden. With forbidden fruit. Forbidden...
>(There is a knock on the door. Both look slightly surprised. They separate, and ANNA goes to a window overlooking the walk where the doorway is)

Ah. The serpents have arrived. I'll go get an apple. And some coffee.
>(Knocking again. SEBASTIAN gives ANNA a look of slight annoyance, as ANNA leaves the room and he answers the door. Leipzig Church Council Members, DR. BORN and MRS. WOLFF enter)

SEBASTIAN
Welcome, my friends. Please come in.

DR. BORN
Thank you, Herr Bach.
>(They bow to one another. SEBASTIAN bows back, and offers to take the MRS. WOLFF'S cloak)

MRS. WOLFF
No, thank you, Herr Bach. We are not to stay long.

SEBASTIAN
But Anna is preparing some coffee. Won't you have some? It's French.

MRS. WOLFF
French? Really?

SEBASTIAN
Really.

DR. BORN
Well, I suppose we could.

SEBASTIAN
May I ask why we have the pleasure of such esteemed company?

DR. BORN
We thought we might be more comfortable discussing some...small business matters in this setting. Not so formal.

SEBASTIAN
I see.
>(SEBASTIAN tries to clear a space at the table which is covered in manuscripts)

Here. I am sorry. We are still not exactly unpacked.
>(DR. BORN starts to walk around, while SEBASTIAN seats MRS. WOLFF)

MRS. WOLFF
Thank you. But we wouldn't want to sit where you work.

SEBASTIAN
Not here. I have a study. This is where my children and Anna copy out music.

MRS. WOLFF
Very studious. And convenient to have learned sons and a wife who can do such...tedious work.

SEBASTIAN
Tedious?
>(SEBASTIAN clears off a chair for DR. BORN and placing it at the table)

MRS. WOLFF
All that music. So many parts. Long...and...

SEBASTIAN
Tedious.

MRS. WOLFF
I didn't mean...well, I was trying to say...
>(ANNA enters with a tray of light pastries and a coiffure of coffee)

Ah, Anna Magdalena Bach.

ANNA
Mrs. Wolff. Dr. Born.

DR. BORN
Mrs. Bach.
>(bows, takes ANNA'S hand, and kisses it. ANNA looks a little surprised)

Lovely...eh, pastries.

ANNA
No doubt you have traveled abroad and picked up some foreign customs.

MRS. WOLFF
No doubt.

ANNA
I would invite you to dine with us, but we have been asked to dine with Dr. Deyling. To discuss the Latin classes my husband was to teach. Herr Bach's manner is...
>(speaking Latin "My husband refuses to cooperate. He is very difficult.")

Well, it's "Vir negat ad cooperari. Est agere difficile."

MRS. WOLFF
What is difficult? My Latin is...

DR. BORN
You mean, "Est agere *facile.*" Herr Bach is very easy to get along with. Isn't that right?

ANNA
Of course. Very...easy.

MRS. WOLFF
I am glad. Then what we have to say you will take in a good humor.

DR. BORN
I am afraid, Herr Bach, the church council has some criticism of your recent cantatas.

MRS. WOLFF
More like suggestions.

DR. BORN
More or less along the lines of text. A small adjustment, really. I see you have the Calov Bible Commentary. A scholarly work. It is well worn. Is this where you get your texts?

SEBASTIAN
No. They are taken from the readings from the church's calendar, and those, from the Word of God. Mostly from the Psalms.

DR. BORN
Dark, sad, and suffering words for the most part. I'd say, influenced by the Calov?

SEBASTIAN
Each Sunday's texts are taken straight from the Lutheran calendar.

DR. BORN
But no need to put it *all* in. Why not pick out the happier parts and put that to music?

SEBASTIAN
(growing agitation)
Happier parts of scripture? Am I to pick and choose in that way? Let's keep the "glory hallelujahs" in, but be sure to leave out "woe to me, a wretched sinner?"

MRS. WOLFF
That's it exactly. Like last Sunday's cantata. Much too dark and, oh, operatic. Uplifting at times, but dreadful words. They just don't match. You need to get better words.

SEBASTIAN
The words are from the Holy Scriptures, Mrs. Wolff. What better words am I supposed to find?

ANNA
Oh, Mrs. Wolff, you haven't touched my pastries. And I spent all afternoon folding in the cream.
> (ANNA serves MRS. WOLFF a pastry and almost feeds it to her to stop her)

MRS. WOLFF
Thank you. I do fancy I have an ear for music. But there are many who say your hymns are not...sing-able. You are lucky to have talent to put across such difficult compositions. But when you marry those words to that music, it just drowns out the fun.

SEBASTIAN
Fun?

DR. BORN
What Mrs. Wolff means is that we represent those who are, well, not the aristocracy, but mere citizens. We weren't the ones who championed you. You must know that. It was those whose loyalties are with Augustus the Strong, and whose opinions they follow. We're not as...sophisticated. Just ordinary laymen. We certainly appreciate your talents, but we wanted a Cantor who would just do his job.

SEBASTIAN
I will not teach Latin. I don't have time for such trivial tasks.

MRS. WOLFF
I beg your pardon?

SEBASTIAN
I have employed a deputy for that, and I am paying him out of my own pocket. And as for the music, I am creating well regulated church music for the glory of God and there is no one who will make me produce anything less than the perfection He deserves.

DR. BORN
Perfection? Herr Bach...that is not a very humble...

SEBASTIAN
And to think I am listening to you two judge whether the words of the text are properly married! What do you think I am creating? Bastard children?

DR. BORN
Of course not.
>(SEBASTIAN gets the text of the last Sunday's cantata and drops it on the table)

SEBASTIAN
This is the text from yesterday. Do you remember it?
>(SEBASTIAN hands it to her. She takes it, reluctantly)

"Jesus, Joy of Man's Desiring."
>(SEBASTIAN leans over and turns the manuscript pages to a specific section)

Now, this, here. Read it. What would you suggest I alter?

MRS. WOLF
"Well for me that I have Jesus, O how strong I hold to him…" Hmm. Mmmm. Yes, very nice. Uplifting. But look, here. "When sick and sad am I." And here. "When I feel my heart is breaking." Why so sad? You take us down, when we should be transported up, up, up, into glories. Isn't that your job?

SEBASTIAN
That's it! Only a jackass would complain against this!

>(SEBASTIAN rips the manuscript out of her hands and storms out of the room without a word. ANNA ushers both to door, handing each a pastry)

ANNA
Herr Bach has been working all day and he is very, very tired. You must excuse him. I am sure he will consider all you have suggested for the next cantata.

MRS. WOLFF
I never meant any harm. I hope he is not offended.

ANNA
Not in the least. Thank you, Mrs. Wolff. Merci, Monsieur Born.
>(ANNA returns to the table, smiling. Then while cleaning up, she sings the following words to the tune of the chorale "Jesu, Joy of Man's Desiring.")

ANNA (Cont'd)
"Come, my dear, and enter in and see the serpents all are gone.
You can thank your faithful wife, who stands for you, when you are wrong."
    (SEBASTIAN enters)

SEBASTIAN
I am the jackass.

ANNA
More like a bull. A strong, beautiful statue of a bull. Powerful and immovable.

SEBASTIAN
I should never behave like that. I think if they had heard you sing it as you have now, they never would have had a quarrel. What is so offensive here? What?
    (He paces, reading aloud, as ANNA sits, reciting her own poem)
"Well for me that I have Jesus, O how strong I hold to him that he might refresh my heart, when sick and sad am I." This uplifts. It speaks of deep trust in God.
    (SEBASTIAN reads to himself)

ANNA
    (sitting, reciting, looking at SEBASTIAN)
"what gentle place is this? what holy, silent, restful place where your voice steadies my shaking heart?"

SEBASTIAN
"ah, therefore I will not leave Jesus, when I feel my heart is breaking."
Somber, maybe. A little.
    (reads to himself)

ANNA
"what wisdom, in pools of tears are poured on me, to soothe my fears, when reason weeps and cannot be comforted? you are the magic in my heart. you are the joyful smile on my worried lips."
    (pauses. SEBASTIAN reads to himself, not paying attention to ANNA)

ANNA (Cont'd)
"you are the green, fertile horizon, raised up on my blackened memories of hopelessness, now vanquished by your sunlight, now golden with all the possibilities in the universe, from inside your hands, your fingers, outstretched to me, you give…and give…

SEBASTIAN
"…so I will not leave Jesus, out of heart and face."
    (deeply contemplating what he has just read)

ANNA
"and I receive an immortal song, and I will sing it clear and true, for all the world to hear, and know, I love you."

SEBASTIAN
What, Anna?

ANNA
More coffee?

SEBASTIAN
Coff…oh, yes, thank you. How do you always know what will soothe me?
    (ANNA says nothing. SEBASTIAN looks at the music in his hand)
I can do nothing else but this. This is what I am given to do. Why do they taunt me?

    (ANNA exits with the tray, while SEBASTIAN remains. He puts down that manuscript and picks up the one from earlier and we hear the music from 3rd Aria for the soprano, again, as if moving out of the scene into his own world. The lighting changes to suggest a passage of time, but small. This is the set up for the next scene.)

ACT 1 SCENE 14

(March 21, 1727. SEBASTIAN is composing, seated. After a while ANNA enters. She carries a large, round tin box with many air holes in it, which she carries, with caution, using thick cloths. She places it on the table and opens the top, to reveal many candles, lit, inside. She makes sure all candles are lit, then closes the cover. SEBASTIAN, without looking at it, immediately warms his hands on it, not taking his eyes off a manuscript. ANNA goes out and comes back with a large pile manuscript paper, paper, pens and ink, and a rostrum, trying to balance it all without dropping anything. SEBASTIAN notices, comes to her aid, helping to place them down on the table.)

ANNA
I hope the weight of these manuscripts is no indication of the weightiness of the words.

SEBASTIAN
Should they have the stature of George Frederick Handel, I would be very happy.

ANNA
Large words are fine. But may they be more gracious and welcoming than Herr Handel has been to meeting you.

SEBASTIAN
I will be sure to discuss that with Herr Handel over beer and broth.
(looking over manuscripts)
Picander is doing what I had hoped he would, as the fine librettist he is. What a masterful scoundrel. A poet, a dynamo for work, and very, very provocative.

ANNA
Provocative? Sounds like a perfect description of you, my love.

SEBASTIAN
Yes, we are twins. And did I mention how very wise and gloriously handsome we are?

ANNA
Daily. Do you think he is doing as you, celebrating his birthday by examining texts?

SEBASTIAN
No, he's my doppelganger...an true evil twin. He's drinking and carousing, no doubt.

ANNA
No doubt.
> (ANNA busies herself arranging the table. SEBASTIAN eyes ANNA, as if not wanting to speak, but then speaks without looking at her)

SEBASTIAN
It's gone on too long. He's not a child anymore. You have to put a stop to it.

ANNA
To what, my love?

SEBASTIAN
Friede. Friede and his unhealthy attachment to you.

ANNA
We've...talked.

SEBASTIAN
Talk isn't strong enough. You must discourage him.

ANNA
How? Like you? He needs...

SEBASTIAN
You must put a stop to these unnatural affections. You are not helping him.

ANNA
Neither are you.

(FREIDE & CPE enter. SEBASTIAN remains fixed on reading. BOTH remove heavy coats, lay them on the furniture, going to the candles to warm their hands)

ANNA (Cont'd)
Close the door quickly and take those soaked coats off the furniture!

(FREIDE is hiding a package, and shows ANNA behind SEBASTIAN'S back. ANNA takes it and exits)

CPE
Sorry we're late. We passed the church yard and heard a whole pack of boys roaring with laughter. We climbed up to look over the wall. Don't worry, they never saw us. It was Köpping, and Landvoigt, and Leg, and the rest. You know. Hoffmann, Neucke. They were all imitating the way you scold them for bad singing. "You sing like bleating goats!" And so they do! "Wie ziiit-tern, Und Wan-keeeen!" Like goats stuck in a fence.

(ANNA returns with sweets on a tray. They BOTH try to take a sweet at the same time, as ANNA tries to stop them, but CPE gets one)

ANNA
Not now! These are for later.

CPE
They said this sort of "bad behavior" will end your career as Cantor for sure. You can't take Lutheran hymns which have been sung for hundreds of years and "disguise" them so no one recognizes them. "He must remember he is nothing more than a hired man, not a court composer." They said your organ playing is too complicated and gives them all a royal headache.

FREIDE
Your organ recitals in Dresden were well received. That is a modern city, with modern minds. Not like this ancient tomb. Why couldn't you have gotten a position there?

(FREIDE manages to steal a sweet. ANNA shakes her head)

CPE
And dance music. "What is wrong with the minuet or polonaise," they said? First they complain about changing the hymns and next they want to be dancing the Schuhplatter, slapping their chests and thighs with the peasants.

SEBASTIAN
I am always using dance music. David danced in the streets before the Ark of the Covenant. Dance is a universal power that lifts man's spirit to joyful realms.

FRIEDE
You disguise your dances where they would least expect to find it. Like the sarabande in the final movement of this St. Matthew's Passion. You took that from a dance suite for solo flute. I remembered it, because I once copied it out.
    (indicates a manuscript)
I copied it out a second time, here, but now it has been slowed down and used for a completely different text. A moment of revelation. "Truly, this man was God's own Son." A revelation with sorrow and…regret. Deep regret, because he was one of those who crucified Him.

SEBASTIAN
You are very perceptive. You see things where others don't. It causes much grief. This seeing. Will they never have enough of judging me? But I won't let them slow this stallion down. Come.
    (setting up the manuscripts on the table to be copied out)
Just a few weeks until Good Friday service. Between now and then we will need Divine intervention to make it sound like music at all.

ANNA
We will not do any work!

SEBASTIAN
What?

ANNA
We will not do work until you let us celebrate this very important occasion.

CPE
We need to celebrate your birthday so we can sing like goats in your honor.

ANNA
Friede and Carl have something special for you.
    (ANNA gets the package and gives it to FRIEDE)

CPE
Something only a pope or king would own.

FRIEDE
We won't tell you where it's from because you would guess it right off. But here's a hint. It's as fragrant as incense rising up to God's throne, and equally pleasurable for a man.

CPE
You're giving it away!

SEBASTIAN
No, I don't have a clue.

FRIEDE
Happy birthday, father.

    (FRIEDE hands SEBASTIAN package. FRIEDE embraces SEBASTIAN, who at first is a little startled, but then embraces him back. He sniffs and shakes gift)

CPE
Come on, father! Open it.

    (SEBASTIAN opens it. It is a fancy clay pipe and a pouch of tobacco)

SEBASTIAN
This is most unexpected!

FRIEDE
It's from Bavaria. That pipe is rumored to have been used by Maximilian the First. The tobacco comes from the colonies in the New World.

SEBASTIAN
This is too much. The cost alone. How did you manage it?

FRIEDE
Picander helped. He was in Rome and found a way to get it. Smoking has become a great enterprise in Italy. Pope Benedict XIII smokes and uses snuff. He's repealed all the papal bulls against clerical smoking.

SEBASTIAN
No doubt he received that order straight from the smoke clouds about God's throne.
    (takes it out, examines it carefully and pens the pouch, smells it, and is delighted)
Extraordinary gift.

ANNA
Now my turn. I have a...a kind of gift for you. Here.
    (she gets her Notebook, carrying it to the harpsichord)
You created this book for me so that I might learn to play well. Well enough for your discerning ears, anyway. Well. Now I will play something for you. From my Notebook.
    (ANNA plays the Minuet in G Major (Christian Petzold.) She struggles, but does a decent job. SEBASTIAN is enraptured by her. ALL applaud her at the end)

SEBASTIAN
My angel. My little round Italian cherub!
    (SEBASTIAN kisses her fondly. FRIEDE finds this difficult and turns away)

CPE
Why did you pick one in your Notebook which isn't by father?

ANNA
Because it was the easiest one for me to learn. Herr Petzold's is much easier than any of your father's. But even in attempting that, I am very much the amateur.

SEBASTIAN
Sing, Anna.

ANNA
What? No. Not now.

SEBASTIAN
You want to please me for my birthday? Then sing "Bist du Bei Mir." Sing it and Friede will play it. He's played it once before, a long time ago. And very well. Remember?

ANNA
Yes. Yes, I do

FRIEDE
Then sing it.

CPE
But that's not yours either.

SEBASTIAN
Let's hear an angel sing it, while we are moved to dance into the "heavenlies."

CPE
Yes, dance!

ANNA
Alright, alright. Take it out and I will give it a try.
(CPE gets Anna's Notebook, FRIEDE sits at harpsichord, ANNA moves to it)
You know I haven't really sung since, well, two years ago when I sang at the Weissenfels Court for the birthday of Duke Christian. That was your first version of the Easter Oratorio. I do miss being the songbird.
(CPE has found the piece and opens to it, placing it on the harpsichord. Anna moves around behind FRIEDE to see the words. FRIEDE plays it beautifully as ANNA sings it (about 1/3 – 1/2 of the piece. Marilyn Horne/Bist du Bei Mir. At the end, CPE and SEBASTIAN applaud. ANNA curtseys and FRIEDE stands and bows. It is a pleasant moment. Then SEBASTIAN turns away, as if stricken by something)

SEBASTIAN
It's too much, really. You are too....such memories. I am overcome.

(SEBASIAN sits. ANNA goes to him, but he is warding her off. FRIEDE is watching this and seems rather disturbed by it. He sits down and starts playing again, but this time he plays the Musette, BWV Anhang 126. He plays it very fast)

CPE
So the competition has begun, has it?
(ANNA is watching SEBASTIAN. FRIEDE stops playing. CPE sits down next to him, but FRIEDE won't let him play, but instead FRIEDE plays his music from his Notebook. BWV 836, Allemande in G minor (1). Possibly composed by Wilhelm Friedemann Bach or BWV 837, Allemande in G minor (2). Possibly composed by Wilhelm Friedemann Bach. Plays fast, stops halfway)

FRIEDE
Top that.

CPE
That's yours from your notebook. That isn't fair.

FRIEDE
Then play something by Father in the new notebook.
(CPE tries to take the Notebook, but FRIEDE takes it away from him)
From memory.

CPE
Alright.
(CPE plays Bach: Polonaise-Menuet-March, and stops in the middle)
Now you finish it.

FRIEDE
I can't. I don't know it well enough to…

CPE
Then this.
(Plays Minuet in F Major, BWV Anh. 113 as ANNA turns completely and is watching them intently)

FRIEDE

I can play that in my sleep.

> (FRIEDE sits next to CPE and plays it. As they sit side by side, a battle of pieces of Anna's Notebook minuets, taking turns playing a fragment of a piece and daring the other to finish it. SEBASTIAN gets up and wanders past the table. The sound of the harpsichord fades as the lighting changes. ANNA, turns, to watch SEBASTIAN as he moves far away from them, downstage. ANNA, CPE and FRIEDE are now in subdued light. SEBASTIAN stands downstage, facing the audience. We no longer hear the harpsichord, but the sound of the full orchestra for the St. Matthew Passion, leading up to near the end, when the Evangelist is singing, just before the Chorus I & II. "Wahrlich, dieser ist Gottes Sohn Gewesen" (Truly, this man was God's own Son.") Bach- St. Matthew Passion BWV 244 (Karl Richter, 1971) – 20/22. This ends and Sebastian is alone in the light, with all else in darkness.)

SEBASTIAN

Soli Deo Gloria. Forgive me.

> (Lights down)

ACT 1 SCENE 15

(Anna is copying out music. She has many pages, pens and ink and a rastrum. She stops, smiles, as if bemused by something. She takes out her poetry manuscript book and begins to write in it. She seems enraptured by what she has written, however briefly. She has run out of ink. She stops, lays down her manuscript open on the table and exits. SEBASTIAN enters almost immediately. He moves to the table and notices the music manuscript, picking it up and looking it over. He then notices ANNA's book, picks it up and begins to read. As he does, he is becoming both emotional and agitated. ANNA returns)

SEBASTIAN
(holding up the poems)
What are these? You left them out. You were copying out this music...but...

ANNA
I didn't expect you for hours.

SEBASTIAN
Obviously.

ANNA
Yes, yes. And I was inspired once again to write...about you.

SEBASTIAN
Inspired?

ANNA
I was afraid of this. Your reaction. Your storms.

SEBASTIAN
More love poems.

ANNA
So they are. And every word is the truth. I can't see what is wrong with expressing my love for my husband. Poets have written about this for centuries. I write what I feel. And I feel all this for you.

SEBASTIAN

I know. I know.

ANNA

You wrote me a poem for our wedding day. "Your slave am I, sweet maiden bride, God give you joy this morning! The wedding flowers, your tresses hide, To dress your form's adorning. Oh how with joy my heart is filled, To see your beauty blooming, Till all my soul with music's thrilled, My heart's with joy...o'erflowing." Was that all a lie? A terrible exaggeration?

SEBASTIAN

Every word was...is perfect. It is who you are to me.

ANNA

Then what is it?

SEBASTIAN

I've told you how I've felt about this. All of this....look at it. This is too much.

ANNA

Too much what? Love?

SEBASTIAN

This isn't love...this....is worship. No man should receive this much...

ANNA

Passion? It is my Song of Solomon. My Song of Sebastian. I adore you.

SEBASTIAN

That's it! That's what I mean. No man should get this kind of....of....

ANNA

Love?

SEBASTIAN

Stop using that word. This love is misguided. This kind of devotion should be only for God.

ANNA
I didn't marry God. I married you. Why are you so angry when I write so plainly about how I love you? There is more to this. What is it?
(pause)
Does it have to do with Maria Barbara? Friede told me. How you acted when you came back from Leopold's court after she was gone. You said a lot without meaning to, I suppose. You muttered things. He was listening, Sebastian. He's angry because he feels you abandoned her for...

SEBASTIAN
What more does God want from me?

ANNA
Maybe for you to let it go. Let go of whatever is plaguing you.

SEBASTIAN
You have to stop this. You have to.

ANNA
I don't understand.

SEBASTIAN
I ran to the Prince's court to play like a child in a nursery. I was so pompous. I wanted to take what was my high, important, deserved place in the sun. Or so I thought. I left Maria Barbara behind, and I made the choice to please an earthly king above God. So He punished me for my idolatry by taking away my wife.

ANNA
That's not so. That's crazy. It's just not so.

SEBASTIAN
When you write these...it's too strong. It becomes idolatry and needs to be dealt with.

ANNA
(stops for a moment, and then gets it)
You're afraid God will take me away.
(SEBASTIAN won't answer)
You won't lose me because I love you too much, whether I have written it down, here, or on the tablets of my heart.

SEBASTIAN
Please, Anna. Please. Don't love me too much.
> (SEBASTIAN exits. ANNA is at first confused and angry, but then picks up her book and holds it, looking it over, embraces it)

ANNA
My joy, my love. You are the very fabric of my dreams. When I embrace you, I embrace all life, not death. God, forgive me, but I **will** love you too much.

> (ANNA exits with her book)

ACT 1 SCENE 16

(November 21, 1728. Music used during scene: J. S. Bach - Cantata "Weinen, Klagen, Sorgen, Zagen" BWV 12 - 2. Weinen, Klagen, Sorgen, Zagen (2/7) (Weeping, Lamenting, Worrying, Fearing) **2. Chorus:** Weeping, lamentation, worry, despair, anguish and trouble are the Christian's bread of tears, that bear the marks of Jesus. We are in the church, where SEBASTIAN is seated on a very uncomfortable chair outside of a door which leads to room in which the Church Council meets. It is below the organ and choir loft. Lights come up slowly, as SEBASTIAN sits, and we can hear what is being said behind the closed door)

VOICE OF COURT COUNCILOR STEGER
It should be remembered that when the Cantor had come hither he had received a dispensation concerning teaching. Magister Pezold had attended to the functions poorly enough, but the Cantor was to take care of at least one of the lowest classes and he has not conducted himself as he should. Moreover, without the foreknowledge of the burgomaster in office, the Cantor sent a choir student to the country, who went away without obtaining leave. This is an offense which the Cantor must be reproached and admonished.

VOICE OF COURT COUNCILOR LANGE
I want to inform the Council that everything is true that has been mentioned against the Cantor, and he should be admonished, and his place filled with Magister Kriegel.

VOICE OF COURT COUNCILOR STEGER
Not only did the Cantor do nothing, but he was not even willing to….
(Door opens and SUPERINTENDENT DR. DEYLING exits the room and SEBASTIAN rises. DEYLING goes to SEBASTIAN)

DEYLING
Ah, Kapellmeister.

SEBASTIAN
Cantor. That is my title, is it not?

DEYLING
Yes.

SEBASTIAN
Then, good evening Superintendent Dr. Deyling. I didn't know they called you to this inquisition.

DEYLING
No, I decided to come on my own volition. I wanted to know what forms of torture they were devising for their heretic Cantor.

SEBASTIAN
I wouldn't be surprised if they used that word against me as well. They have used every other. Tell me. Is the Rector present?

DEYLING
Present for this? No, he wouldn't be here for such insignificant...

SEBASTIAN
Yes, to him my affairs with the council would be insignificant.

DEYLING
My dear Kapell...Cantor. Herr Ernesti can do as he pleases. He may be old in both his years and his ways, but he does have the ear of the council. You would do well to stop antagonizing and crossing him. You are fire and he is water. Can you begin to understand this?

SEBASTIAN
On this point you have bought me into the light, Dr. Deyling

DEYLING
I mean to bring you out of your present darkness.

SEBASTIAN
Oh, but I love darkness. The brightness of the day interferes with the "light" that guides me. I compose mostly at night so that my own light may be dim and the light of Christ illuminate what I am to write...not for the glory of man, but for the glory of God.

DEYLING
Yes, of course. All for the glory of God.

SEBASTIAN
Yes.

DEYLING
They talk on and on about nothing, and all before supper. It is guaranteed their stomachs will end their debate soon.

SEBASTIAN
All the better. Mine is grumbling, too. It is late and I wish for my supper as well.

DEYLING
How is your dear wife and family?

SEBASTIAN
We are well.

DEYLING
Surely, you *lie* well.

SEBEASTIAN
You are right. Five years of...little lives gone, as if they never were.

DEYLING
I heard about your many losses in such a short time.

SEBASTIAN
Two years ago this June 29th, my sweet, dancing Christina Sophia Henrietta. Five years of bright sunlight, extinguished. November 1st, last year, darling Ernestus Andreas, barely a month old. September 21st of this year, Christian Gottlieb, my three year old genius. He was playing the flute at two.

DEYLING
I am truly sorry.

SEBASTIAN
Anna is the one who keeps me focused. If she didn't ground me in the here and now, I would be off into the third heaven without a rope to tether me to reality.
> (Music starts above, as a choir sings. It is as if it is coming from above in the choir loft, so both men look up, pausing to listen.)

DEYLING
New singers?

SEBASTIAN
Yes, and barely enough.

DEYLING
Who is leading them? Krebs?

SEBASTIAN
No, Krause.

DEYLING
He has them off to a good start.

SEBASTIAN
Passable.

DEYLING
But he is appointed by you.

SEBASTIAN
His proficiency is good, but he is too harsh in his manner.

DEYLING
Unlike you, his master?

SEBASTIAN
I am a hard man, yes. But I am fair. He will learn.
    (Music stops and then starts again at the beginning. They listen again for a moment, and then talk as it is being sung)

DEYLING
"Weep. Lamentation. Worry. Despair. Anguish and trouble are the Christian's bread of tears." Interesting words. You are a master at the truly depressive and dark.

SEBASTIAN
It speaks exactly to the point I wish to express.

DEYLING
And that is exactly your problem, Kapellmeister.

SEBASTIAN
Cantor.

DEYLING
No. Kapellmeister. Let us call you what you are, truly. You have held that title from Cöthen, have you not? The others may not be willing to admit to it, but I am. You are truly a master above them all. Why then do you cause those exposed to your genius to be filled with deep melancholy? There is, oh, so much pounding and weeping and lamentations. Shall we all suffer the suffering of Christ so vividly every Sunday?

SEBASTIAN
But the sounds, Dr. Deyling. Listen. Listen beyond the words.
    (indicates above them)
There...there is more peace and joy and love and light in one, long, crying note for the Almighty, than in a thousand jingling, jangling tunes with happy words to satisfy the mob.
    (Music stops again. Voices from the room are heard)

VOICE OF COURT COUNCILOR STEGER
Herr Ernesti will object to that, you know very well. The Cantor is incorrigible. Must he be granted this permission?

VOICE OF COURT COUNCILOR LANGE
Of course. It is only proper. But where is Dr. Deyling?

VOICE OF COURT COUNCILOR STEGER
What does it matter? We have enough here to vote on it right now. The Vice-Chancellor and Burgomaster, Dr. Born, is here.

VOICE OF COURT COUNCILOR LANGE
Put it to a vote then.
    (Music starts from above, drowning out the council voices)

DEYLING
They must be very hungry if they are voting this soon.

SEBASTIAN
Why did they call me here if they are going to end the meeting so abruptly?

DEYLING

Don't you know? Then you haven't heard. My poor man. I would have told you if I thought you didn't know.

SEBASTIAN

Know what?
> (DR. BORN comes out and looks for SEBASTIAN. Music continues above)

DR. BORN

Oh, there you are, Cantor. I am sorry we have made you wait this long, but we were in debate much longer than we had anticipated. We were hoping we could discuss with you how long you will need to be away.

SEBASTIAN

Away for what?

DEYLING

He doesn't know.

DR. BORN

Oh, this is terrible. Why didn't anyone tell him? Cantor, I have most difficult news for you. Your Prince, Prince Leopold of Anhalt-Cöthen, is dead.
> (Music from above moves into a more lively section of this same piece as SEBASTIAN is taking in that fact. He reels back a little and then sits here he had been sitting before)

His son by his second wife died of smallpox in August and his daughter, too, succumbed to it and died this September. It is reported that the Prince, overcome with grief and no heirs, must have been weakened and succumbed to smallpox, himself, and passed on from this world to be with his God on the 19th of November, just two days ago. Devastating news. I know he was both your prince and friend.

SEBASTIAN

More than a brother.

DR. BORN
His funeral will no doubt take place within the next months. They will want you for a funerary cantata, I am sure. And singers. We are prepared to release the choir to you, but other musicians you will have to find yourself. We are prepared to grant you leave for all of this.

SEBASTIAN
(barely listening)
More than…oh, poor Anna. Now all hope is gone.

DEYLING
Hope for what?

SEBASTIAN
For ever going back.
(Music swells again with the lighter and brighter music as the choir sings. Lights fade while SEBASTIAN remains still, while the others exit.)

END OF ACT 1

Passions – Karen Klami

ACT 2 SCENE 1

INTERMISSION AND JUST BEFORE RISE FOR ACT 2:
We hear the music of St. John's Passion, excerpts.

WHILE STAGE IS DARK, AS LIGHTS COME UP VERY SLOWLY:
Opening of the second act, as the room is dark, before lights are up, we hear the music from Cantata BWV, 105, Aria III.

III. Aria (Soprano): "Wie zittern und wanken, die Sünder Gedanken" (How they tremble and waver, the thoughts of the sinners), Ton Koopman - Trinity IX Sunday, "Herr, gehe nicht ins Gericht mit deinem Knect," BWV 105, July 25, 1723. The oboe introduction is heard, and then the singer sings (in German):
"How they tremble and waver, The thoughts of the sinners, In that they do often accuse one another. And then turn around and would dare make excuses.
Just so is the scrupulous conscience. Because of its own torments shattered."

> (We hear the music of Aria III of cantata BWV sung from up above, as if from the "heavenlies." A soprano, lit "angelically" as possible, can be actually singing with a live orchestra or piped in orchestra, or she can be lip-synching with piped in music. She is the only thing lit for a while, but as the music continues, lights come up very slowly, as the singing fades. March 24, 1729. Leopold's entombment with the funeral music at St. Jacob's performed by Bach. New text by Picander (p. 236). The lights come up on ANNA, in her best court clothing, is seated near FRIEDE, who is seated at a harpsichord. They are both facing audience, with FRIEDE slightly facing at an angle, as if a part of an unseen, offstage orchestra. The upstage background behind them is St. Jacob's, a large gothic, tall, stone structure, dark, and with a London bridge looking two towers connecting a small span outside of it.
> SEBASTIAN is standing to one side, facing slightly toward offstage. We will hear the music below, which is being played by FRIEDE and off stage musicians. SEBASTIAN is conducting them from downstage, facing upstage, slightly to one side. A PRIEST in robes enters, and stands to one side, raising his arms as if in benediction, while is chanting a cappella, in Latin. He now speaks)

PRIEST
And so, we do now, today, this day, the 24th day of our Lord, seventeen hundred twenty-nine, lay to rest our beloved despot, our Prince among earthly princes, Prince Leopold of Anhalt-Cöthen, who served his Lord and Savior, Jesus Christ, with all dutiful devotion and loyalty to the church, and with humility and grace. His worthy Kapellmeister, Herr Johann Sebastian Bach, has composed music as is befitting a monarch's reign and for the glory of God. And so, on this day, we will now be reminded of our benevolent and kindly prince.
(The PRIEST moves offstage, as SEBASTIAN steps up to conduct by moving downstage and facing slightly to ones side, facing ANNA and FRIEDE. SEBASTIAN starts the conducting, with FREIDE playing the harpsichord, with ANNA seated. The piece starts and continues for a short time.

> **Funeral Music BWV 244a / n ° 24 –** *Die Augen sehn nach deiner Leiche*
> *(The eyes look after your body)* – like opening of B Minor Mass.
>
> This quickly fades, as the following comes up, with SEBASTIAN having stopped conducting, turning to face the audience, as if enraptured.
>
> **Funeral Music BWV 244a / n ° 10 – Erhalte mich (Get me)** - like St. Matthew Passion.
>
> This fades as SEBASTIAN turns back upstage and watches, as a vision of PRINCE LEOPOLD, accomplished by the lighting on him, in his usual clothing, as we have seen him in Act 1, and carrying his Viola da Gamba, seen only by SEBASTIAN, walks upstage and sits down at a chair. We can see LEOPOLD as he is not blocked by SEBASTIAN due to a slight raising of the area or in some other way. The music fades completely as LEOPOLD starts to play the Viola de Gamba as a solo.
>
> **J.S. Bach: Sonata for Viola de Gamba and Harpsichord BWV 1027, Adagio.**
> SEBASTIAN watches, his back to the audience. Behind LEOPLOD, where he is playing, and behind ANNA and FRIEDE, emerges a kind of portal or opening (Stargate) like a heavenly

opening, which suggests a gate or door, but is hard to really define, as from there emits extraordinary light and it is difficult to see any definable object. This light will change with each musical piece that is heard, so that it resembles a heavenly emitted light show. Coming from this portal we hear the sound of each piece of music, flowing one into the other, as one comes up, plays, and fades, as the next comes up, and fades, etc. It is a flow as in a medley of music in the composer's mind which is past, present and future. It has no chronological order. It is an epiphany, glorious beyond measure to SEBASTIAN. It is a door from Heaven opening up so that he hears it all, like a vision in sonority, and is transported into the "heavenlies." It starts with LEOPOLD playing, but he disappears due to the great light that emits from the portal, and he leaves the stage, not seen again. The music transitions into the following order, quickly, moving from one recognizable theme to the next. Only small excerpts are used for fast flow:

Pablo Casals: Bach Cello Solo No. 1, BWV 1007

Brandenburg Concertos (1721)
Orchestra of the Enlightenment Brandenburg Concerto No. 3 – I Allegro BWV 1048, Karl Munchinger, 1951: Brandenburg Concerto No. 5 in D Major, BWV 1050 (Allegro).

The St. Matthew Passion (1727) – Opening
Willem Mengelberg (my personal favorite)
or use
Carl Richter – 1/22
then
Carl Richter - 41 Mache dich, mein Herze rein

Goldberg Variations (1741-1742)
Glenn Gould – Aria (piano)
Variation 1 BWV 988 (harpsichord)

St .John Passion (1723) – Opening
Get to 1:04 and the singing as quickly as possible

Air on a G String
Overture, Suite No. 3 in D Major "Air" BWV 1068 (1729)

Italian Concerto (1735)
Wanda Landowska – Italian Concerto BWV 971, 3rd Movement (Presto) (Pleyel harpsichord),

Magnificat in D Major (1731)

Christmas Oratorio (1734)
Cantata #1 BWV 248 Movement 1/9,

The Well-Tempered Clavier (Book 1 and 2, 1742)
Fugue No. 2 in C Minor BWV 847 (WTC 1)
or
Wanda Landowska – Fugue No. 2 in C Minor BWV 847 (WTC 1)

The Musical Offering (1747)
Musikalisches Opfer BWV 1079 (1/6)

The Art of the Fugue (unfinished, 1749)
Glenn Gould – Contrapunctus IV
The Art of Fugue, BWV 1080 – T. Koopman and T. Mathot
Cannon II

B Minor Mass (1724)
ONLY USE
Joshua Rifkin – B Minor Mass
Kyrie
Gloria
ending with *Crucifixus*

As this last piece plays out, the lighting of the portal closes and it is as it was in the beginning. ANNA is still seated and FRIEDE is at the harpsichord, as if nothing at all out of the ordinary has happened. At the end of it, SEBASTIAN is down on his knees, facing upstage, head bowed)

PRIEST'S VOICE

We thank our Lord God, our Heavenly Father and King, for His most holy and perfect will for our lives in this world, whatever difficulties are presented to us, and are contrary to our own wills, that we may be found worthy in humility, and through the grace of Jesus Christ, we may be found faultless, and enter into His eternal glory. Amen.

(SEBASTIAN is now prostrate on the floor. Lights down slowly to blackout)

ACT 2 SCENE 2

> (October, 1731. Bach home. SEBASTIAN and MIZLER are seated at the table with manuscript pages in large piles all over and rostrums and various music copying devices of the day are also strewn about. SEBASTIAN lights his pipe)

SEBASTIAN
Alright. I will make this as plain and clear as possible. Every good and creative thought I think is only through the grace of God. Every jot, every tittle, is released through me, a mere conduit of the Holy Spirit's desire to express Himself. On a good day, I take it down as fast as I can. The experience is better than anything found in life or death or angels or demons or hell itself freezing over.
> (He takes a pose, puffing out a large puff of smoke from his pipe)

MIZLER
And on a bad day?

SEBASTIAN
On a bad day, my friend, Mizler....I sigh and rehearse the choir.
> (CPE enters whistling the Harpsichord Concerto in C minor BWV 1060, Adagio Theme, followed by FRIEDE. They ramble around looking at manuscripts)

FREIDE
Mizler! What are you doing here already? I just spent the better part of the last hour looking for you at the coffeehouse.

MIZLER
The Kapellmeister wished more copiers for his music, so I was "enlisted."

SEBASTIAN
Accosted. He is good and fast, and owes me for the ale I purchased for him at Zimmermann's last Thursday.

FREIDE
We are planning a trip to Dresden to hear the opera. All three of us.

SEBASTIAN
Three?

CPE
Yes. I am planning to go.

SEBASTIAN
It is a wearying trip for such little songs.

CPE
I want to hear them.

FRIEDE
"Shall we go to Dresden again and hear their beautiful little songs?" Your words.

SEBEASTIAN
The arias of Hasse's work are beautiful and I used to like to go, but no longer. Things are changing there.

MIZLER
New philosophies bring new art.

SEBASTIAN
I thought it was the other way round. The artist on the vanguard of God's next inspiration. From a man's soul, perhaps we may get music that has the emotional power to link the soul to the heaven.

MIZLER
The soul is for the church, and the mind, for the world.

SEBASTIAN
For whom do you compose? The church or the world?

MIZLER
The world. And you?

SEBASTIAN
Both.

MIZLER
How?

SEBASTIAN
As a prophet. The office of Asaph, King David's Kapellmeister, was both musician and prophet. That is what the Book of Psalms gives us. The voice of God, Almighty…to man…almighty. Kings and priests, alike. The secular and religious worlds are one.

MIZLER
How can you say that? That doesn't make any sense.

SEBASTIAN
"There are more things in heaven and earth, Horatio, than are dreamt of in your philosophy." From a play by an Englishman who wrote for queen and kinfolk.

CPE
Well put, Father.

MIZLER
Then you agree with him?

CPE
I agree with…what I agree with.

MIZLER
So much for free thinkers in the Bach clan.

CPE
What is this? I can't get it out of my mind.
   (whistles Harpsichord Concerto in C minor BWV 1060, Adagio Theme)

FRIEDE
It is what we are going to perform next Thursday. The Concerto in C.

SEBASTIAN
Did he get the two harpsichords?

FRIEDE

I talked with Zimmermann and he assured me they will be there. He acquired these especially for us to use. One is a Hieronymus Albrecht Hass, and the other, French. A Blanchet. There was much arguing and debate, but he procured them.

SEBASTIAN
(holding up a manuscript)

I was considering this for the week following. Just this part.

FRIEDE

A cantata? That's mixing it up for the crusty merchants and town drunks who won't darken the door of the church.

SEBASTIAN

Tobacco, ale, coffee and pastries bring them in, through their stomachs. While they enrich their bodies, once in a while, why can't I enrich their souls?

CPE

Sneaky.

MIZLER

Unethical.

FRIEDE

Hilarious.

SEBASTIAN

Aside from the town burgomaster, some of those drunks are the best ears passing through Leipzig and know a good tune when they hear it. We are establishing side by side a pleasing harmony of sounds...and, I hope, a meeting of minds.

CPE

I would like to play one of these there within the month. But which one?
(CPE plays a part of each: Solo per il cembalo in E-flat major, BWV Anh. 129, March in D major, BWV Anh. 122, Polonaise in G minor, BWV Anh. 123, March in G major, and BWV Anh. 124)

FRIEDE
I prefer the March in D Major.

MIZLER
Are they all your own compositions, Carl?

CPE
Yes...but I stole the style!

FRIEDE
We have our own style.

SEBASTIAN
Come, Carl. I need your good manuscript hand. I want you to start on this too.
    (CPE stops and SEBASTIAN hands them a manuscript)
B minor mass...an oratorio for Christmas. But for the coffeehouse....I don't know if we will have enough singers for this. I need six strong soloists.

FRIEDE
    (comes over to SEBASTIAN and looks over his shoulder)
We have plenty for these. But where will we get a decent bass? And here...let's hope some trumpeters from out of town breeze through for a listen and are moved to join in.

CPE
Thank God for the Collegium Musicum. Total control and room to breathe.

FRIEDE
Yes, we all can breathe there.

MIZLER
With the exception of me.

FRIEDE
How so?

MIZLER

You recreate your *father's* music in your own.
    (FRIEDE is about to protest)
Oh, no. I don't mean it isn't yours in the end. I am looking to the enlightened new tastes. Sounds coming from sweet, *human* nectar. You have all the most gifted university students performing and composing. I see this as the Collegium Musicum's perfect opportunity to introduce this new kind of music to the public.

SEBASTIAN

You call it sweet? Are you so ready to drink sweet nectar in every composition? I'd rather have some strong ale.

MIZLER

You may find that if you don't change some of your own music, you may lose your whole following.

SEBASTIAN

I won't be dragged in. If I decide to be an idiot, then I will be an idiot on my accord.
    (CPE & FRIEDE laugh, but try to hide it when they see MIZLER is not amused)

MIZLER

Are you insulting me, Kapellmeister?

SEBASTIAN

Surely not! It is most *intelligent* for a man to follow himself blindly if he agrees with his own strong opinion.

MIZLER

You *are* making fun of me.

SEBASTIAN

Just making sport of such serious modern opinions. Where is your sense of fun? "If the tune too labored ring, And the mouth in bondage sing, It will waken naught for sport."

CPE

That's sounds familiar. Is that what you are copying out?
    (picking up the manuscript that MIZLER was copying)
The Dramma per Musica, *The Contest Between Phoebus and Pan.*

MIZLER
Doesn't sound like a religious work.

SEBASTIAN
No, it is actually my…secular, political *and* philosophical statement. From my mind, directly to the mind of Herr Scheibe.

MIZLER
An intellectual battle, then?

SEBASTIAN
Precisely. I am Phoebus, and Herr Scheibe is Pan. There is a musical contest and Phoebus wins because his music, mine, is judged "good." And Pan's music is judged "bad." Someone's ears get turned into a donkey's. And so forth and so on. The end.

MIZLER
I am bound to agree with Herr Scheibe, and side with Pan. But still, I would be happy to copy out such a work.

SEBASTIAN
No. I have called you to copy out something of extraordinary value. A gem straight from the natural mind of man.
    (Hands MIZLER the music. He reads the title to himself, then reacts, half laughing and half annoyed. CPE picks it up, reads the title to himself and laughs)

CPE
Ein fest Burg ist Usen Gott. A Mighty Fortress is Our God. This arrangement is huge. Is this for the Reformation Day celebration?

SEBASTIAN
Yes.

MIZLER
You continue to mock me, Kapellmeister.

SEBASTIAN
No, I don't think I do. You do it to yourself.

MIZLER
The new music is full of elegant simplicity because it is "natural." And what is called genius is nothing more than science and mathematics at work. Calculate the effects of chords and melodies on the soul, and on the basis of these results, establish esthetic rules for composition. Herr Wolff in his philosophies has said that by seeing this, it is the only way to distinguish true miracles from fictitious.

SEBASTIAN
Are there miracles that are *not* true? Minds are a cesspool of deception. There is no trusting the mind of man.

MIZLER
But through our minds we can lift genius and musical instinct from its dark prison of subjectivity into the light of reason.

SEBASTIAN
And what about love? Where is the light of reason in love? Can the mind comprehend it mathematically? Isn't it like a riddle canon? The first voice comes in, singing, but alone. It is only when another voice is welcomed, and searches, calculating for a place to enter, that the canon is revealed as a whole. Complete.
    (ANNA enters from outdoors, carrying a package, taking off her cloak and hat)

ANNA
Good afternoon, gentlemen. I hope Herr Kapellmeister hasn't been too stingy with the heat and frozen off your busy fingers.
    (ALL are quiet and don't respond)
I see he has. Are your mouths are all frozen as well?

SEBASTIAN
Good afternoon, my *beloved*.
    (ALL say nothing, uncomfortable. ANNA stops, puzzled, then continues)

ANNA
Something hot? That will warm you, body and soul, I pray.
    (ANNA smiles and exits, still puzzled)

SEBASTIAN
Love. One needs unusual abilities to solve this riddle. Abilities reaching far beyond the mathematical mind.

MIZLER
Clearly I am not the man for the task.

SEBASTIAN
Then you will find yourself utterly alone in your reasonable and enlightened world.

(Lights down)

ACT 2 SCENE 3

(Early 1732. ANNA is singing, while SEBASTIAN plays the harpsichord or clavichord. He is accompanying her as she sings "Laudamus te" (We praise thee, We worship thee, We glorify thee) from the B Minor Mass, (Joshua Rifkin). SEBASTIAN plays, and stops in fits and starts, scribbling on the manuscript before them. He begins to play and ANNA starts to sing, but in the wrong place)

SEBSASTIAN
No! This isn't the...Start here. Here!
(SEBASTIAN plays, giving her a measure before as an introduction. ANNA starts singing again, but after a short time, SEBASTIAN stops and scribbles)

ANNA
Maybe you should do this alone, as you usually do.

SEBASTIAN
No! No. I need to hear your voice.

ANNA
Why?

SEBASTIAN
It is a comfort.

ANNA
Comfort? Seems like more of an irritation, at least as I am experiencing it.

SEBASTIAN
I'm sorry. I am so used to hearing it sung by such goats. Please sing it.

ANNA
Not now. Time to rest us both.

SEBASTIAN
Not yet. I have to get...this...

(seems to have thought of something and goes back to the music. ANNA sits)

ANNA
She would have been one years old tomorrow. Christina Dorothea. Born at the very stroke of 10:00, according to the gonging parlor clock. Funny how I remember that.
(SEBASTIAN stops and looks, but says nothing)
Christina Benedicta Louise would be almost three. Christian Gottlieb, seven. Ernestus Andreas, let's see…not quite five. Christina Sophia Henrietta would have been…

SEBASTIAN
Oh, Anna.

ANNA
No. No, it is alright. They're all in heaven, are they not?
(SEBASTIAN goes back to his manuscript)
I don't think I will be going to Hägenstrasse to shop any longer.

SEBASTIAN
And why is that?

ANNA
Too many voices whispering and eyes darting back and forth between women as I pass. Great gossipers, these women of Leipzig. What do they take me for? I can hear most of it as I pass. They are hiding it less and less.
(imitates them)
"The Cantor's wife is pregnant *again*? Now, how many is it that she has lost? She's like his lap dog. Too small, with too few nipples to keep her growing litter nourished."

SEBASTIAN
(stops, angrily)
How dare they say such horrors about you?

ANNA
They have said worse, believe me.

SEBASTIAN
I won't let you be subjected to that.

ANNA
How do you propose to stop it?

SEBASTIAN
You're right. I can't. I am sorry. It is a thorn in the flesh. Paul the Apostle prayed fervently that God would remove his, but He wouldn't. I am no better than Paul.

ANNA
Is it me? Am I your thorn?

SEBASTIAN
You? Of course not!

ANNA
Then what is it?

SEBASTIAN
Better I tell no one. Not even you. It is between me and God.

ANNA
Then what is between you and *God* might form a wedge between you and *me*.

SEBASTIAN
That is not so.

ANNA
I don't have your kind of strength. Your kind of trust.

SEBASTIAN
Neither do I. It is a constant struggle not to struggle. Relaxing in faith is the hardest work I have ever been asked to do.

ANNA
I am so frightened.
    (SEBASTIAN embraces her)

SEBASTIAN
I am here.

ANNA
I am pregnant.

SEBASTIAN
How far along?

ANNA
More than three months.

SEBASTIAN
Another gift.

ANNA
A gift to be grabbed back by the sender before long.

SEBASTIAN
If in God's plan, He...

ANNA
It is called, "The Lord giveth and the Lord taketh away." And taketh... Always taking...away. When will the taking be less than the giving? It isn't just the children, Sebastian. It is you. You. What is God doing for you? What do they expect of you?

SEBASTIAN
To be a magician.

ANNA
What?

SEBASTIAN
That is all I am. Look.
    (makes some magician conjuring motions, then sits at the harpsichord)
Yes, Lord? I am listening. What is it? Oh, yes. Here are some notes.
    (plays a chord, then listens)
Yes! And this forms...
    (starts playing an accelerated arpeggio which turns into a complicated piece)
Right before your eyes, like a magician, I have conjured up the music. Straight from the throne.

ANNA
Stop making fun. If they heard you talk like this...This is why they hate you. It's because they cannot comprehend any of it. Sometimes, neither can I. But they are frightened of it....you, and have to destroy you. This is why they all ridicule you.

SEBASTIAN
They do. But do *you*?

ANNA
I don't have the faith for it all. But in you, I put *all* my faith and trust, my love.

SEBASTIAN
Anna, don't. Please. I beg of you. Don't.
  (ANNA plays a chord, then sings "Laudamus te" a cappella.
  SEBASTIAN sits next to her, and plays the music. She stops
  him, taking his hand, and kissing it)
Oh, Anna. How I adore you. I am so sorry...
  (ANNA takes his hand and places it on his mouth to hush him.
  She then takes both of his hands and takes them into her own,
  and gently pulls him up. Facing him, she places both his hands
  on her hips, and then starts dancing with him)

ANNA
I can see and hear what is happening at the holy throne, too, you know. Right now I hear the heavenly choirs singing to the accompaniment of a harp...and a drum...and a lute. They're all dancing up there. All the angels. Can't you see them? Look up. See?
  (SEBASTIAN looks up, as ANNA points. He looks up, pointing)

SEBASTIAN
I see it. A foretaste of heaven. Right...there.
  (ANNA then takes his hand and puts it back on her, then his
  head in her hands, and kisses him on the lips, still dancing.
  SEBASTIAN looks at ANNA)
And...right here.

  (They dance as the lights fade)

ACT 2 SCENE 4

(May, 1733. Bach home. KREBS and KRAUSE are seated. Laughter as the lights come up. FRIEDE and CPE are farthest standing. ANNA is offstage. Music: "Wir Danken dir, Gott, wirdanken dir" BWV 29, Partita in E major BWV 1006)

SEBASTIAN
And so you certainly can't please *people* with your music.

KREBS
Then why compose at all? Isn't music meant to be heard? Who is it for, then?

SEBASTIAN
The aim and final end of all music should be none other than the glory of God and the refreshment of the soul, whether sacred or secular. For instance, after one of my Passions, a noblewoman rushed up to the organ loft. I thought she was eager to praise my work, but then she spoke so all the church could hear:
(in a wobbly old woman's voice)
"Kapellmeister, heaven forbid! What has just taken place in the sanctuary of God...it is as if one was in an opera comedy!"
(all laugh)
Opera comedy or hauptmusik, it is all for Him. I have even reworked music I had for one purpose to serve another. I took the violin solo from my Partita in E Major and worked it into "Wir danken dir, Gott wirdanken dir"...We Thank You God.

KRAUSE
Doesn't that weaken the character of the work, all those changes?

SEBASTIAN
There is nothing weak that comes out when you are tuned into the Almighty.

KREBS
And how does one do *that*?

SEBASTIAN
By simply listening. The voice of God is the very definition of music. Does not nature sing with His voice? The Psalms speak of rocks crying out in songs of praise.

KREBS
Then I will be sure to put my ear close to the next boulder I see, so to be able to tune into the voices of heaven.

SEBASTIAN
You could do worse.

KRAUSE
He does worse in every composition he writes, Herr Kapellmeister.

KREBS
Hey! You look here, you...you organ grinder! He plays like one, you know. And conducts like the organ grinder's monkey. You should see him at rehearsals. Such ape-like moves.
  (KREBS stands and imitates an ape conducting)

KRAUSE
I look like nothing of the sort!

SEBASTIAN
Enough of this foolery. Time to copy out work.

KREBS
Kapellmeister. I have heard that you are changing the words of the great hymns and making them into texts to praise earthly sovereigns. Is this so?

SEBASTIAN
Yes.

KREBS
Isn't that...

SEBASTIAN
Sacrilegious?

KREBS

In a word, yes.

SEBASTIAN

In a word…no.

KREBS

But according to the new philosophies of Wolff and Leibniz…

SEBASTIAN

Sovereigns are worthy of respect for their authority and we do well to honor them in words. In music. However, true praise, in any form, belongs to God, and God alone.

FRIEDE

You would do well to pay attention. He is never wrong in these matters. Most especially, in the matter of such earthly delights as tobacco and coffee. According to father, God drinks His coffee from a great cup made of angels' wings. And His beer from a stein carved from stone taken from the streets of gold. And he smokes His pipe filled with incense of the prayers of the saints.
    (KRAUSE, KREBS and CPE clap. SEBASTIAN is a little put off, but not much)

CPE

Bravo, Friede.

SEBASTIAN

You are quite a poet. I should hire you to write the text for my next cantata.

FRIEDE

With pleasure, mon cher capitan!
    (At this, ANNE enters, carrying a bucket and mop)

ANNA

Ah, you have learned your French well. So, if your father is the captain, I can imagine you are one of his crew. Here, then! Swab the deck!
    (Hands FRIEDE the mop and bucket)

FRIEDE
(takes it with an exaggerated gallantry)
With pleasure, mon cher ami.

ANNA
Ma chère amie. You are the masculine addressing the feminine. French isn't your forte. Just like your father.

FRIEDE
Like him? God forbid!

CPE
Friede!

FRIEDE
I meant no disrespect.

SEBASTIAN
None taken.

FRIEDE
And I mean no disrespect when I say we are to copy out some masterworks that you have taken down, note for note, from some pebbles in the yard. All to the glory of God.

SEBASTIAN
No need to listen to pebbles. But you are right about their purpose.

KRAUSE
What about your works about the joys of smoking and coffee. Do *they* really glorify God?

SEBASTIAN
All music is an agreeable harmony for the honor of God, and the permissible delights of the soul. Tobacco and coffee are some of the most delectable pleasures ever created by God for man. I can easily glorify God all day long with a good pipe and a large draught of coffee. Next to my beloved beer, what else is there better on this earth to inspire?

(CPE sits at the harpsichord and plays an introduction to the recitative of the Coffee Cantata. Need a harpsichord version of this. Bach - Coffee Cantata, at 3:35, Bach: Coffee Cantata, Schweigt stille, plaudert nicht, BWV 211, Part 1 of 2)

CPE
(Recitative, as the character, Schlendrian)
You wicked child, you disobedient girl, oh! when will I get my way; give up coffee!

FRIEDE
(Recitative, as the character, Lieschen, singing in falsetto, funny)
Father, don't be so severe! If I can't drink my bowl of coffee three times daily,
then in my torment I will shrivel up like a piece of roast goat.

ANNA
(Aria, as character, Lieschen)
Mm! how sweet the coffee tastes, more delicious than a thousand kisses, mellower than muscatel wine. Coffee, coffee I must have, and if someone wishes to give me a treat, ah, then pour me out some coffee!
(CPE stops playing. They ALL laugh)

FRIEDE
(going to ANNA)
How the sweet coffee tastes! More delicious than a thousand kisses! I must have it!
(playfully takes her and dances with her. ALL LAUGH except SEBASTIAN)

SEBASTIAN
Anna.
(ANNA & FRIEDE continue dancing)
Anna!
(THEY stop and FRIEDE releases ANNA)
Now then. Be a good Lady Bach and let's have some of that forbidden black nectar of the gods, if you please. For all!
(ANNA exits. KREBS, KRAUSE and CPE applaud)

KRAUSE
You are most kind.

KREBS
Yes, thank you. And some pipe tobacco?

SEBASTIAN

None of that! Not until you are much older. Stunts growth, I have heard it said. You don't want to be half-pints, do you? Where *is* my birthday pipe?

> (CPE goes to the table and retrieves it, but FRIEDE intercepts it and gives it to SEBASTIAN. He takes it from FRIEDE and they exchange a look)

Thank you...my son.

FRIEDE

You are most welcome...my father.

> (SEBASTIAN turns to the others and is jolly)

SEBASTIAN

Drink up! There are barrels full where that comes from. We may be up all the night copying out under the power of strong inspiration... and strong coffee.

> (KREBS and KRAUSE sit at the table, while CPE brings over a lamp and lights it. FRIEDE is staying away from it all at the moment, watching SEBASTIAN light his pipe. ALL get busy at copying. Lights down)

ACT 2 SCENE 5

>(July, 1733. Bach home. ANNA is at the table, reading a letter, which she is making marks upon. SEBASTIAN is at the harpsichord playing the 5th voice part in the Gloria from the Missa (B Minor Mass). He is plays the 5th part melody, and then plays all 5 voices together. He then moves to playing the Kyrie.)

ANNA
I hope that isn't Friede's audition piece.

SEBASTIAN
Why?

ANNA
Too somber.

SEBASTIAN
It is a Kyrie. For the court at Dresden. I am adding it to the Missa in B Minor.

ANNA
A calling card of prominent proportions for a rather prominently proportioned applicant.

SEBASTIAN
In body or head?

ANNA
Both.

SEBASTIAN
This is your doing.

ANNA
I cannot account for your huge head. I do cook the meals. However, I don't force them down your throat.

SEBASTIAN
I am in tight competition with Herr Handel.

ANNA
God forbid!

SEBASTIAN
More of me is better, is it not?
> (She goes to him, puts her arms around him from behind. He continues to play.)

ANNA
It will become a problem, since my arms can't grow any longer.
> (SEBASTIAN stops playing and turns around and pulls ANNA onto his lap)

SEBASTIAN
Bigger lap, though. A better throne upon which to breed.

ANNA
> (gets up, laughing)

The things that come out of you!

SEBASTIAN
I am a scoundrel, it is true. God forgive me for it. But you...I can't help myself.
> (ANNA goes back to the table. SEBASTIAN plays a part of the Gloria again)

ANNA
Your letter to the court is lacking.
> (He stops playing)

Why would they hire a Court Kapellmeister who speaks so crudely?
> (reads)

"I have had the Directorium of the Music in two principal churches in Leipzig, where I have suffered one injury or another. I humbly beg your Highness to favor me concerning the title of Your Highness's Court Capelle..." And so forth. Why not...
> (writing, speaks what she writes, emphasizing her words)

"...but have *innocently* had to suffer....But these injuries would *disappear altogether* if your Royal Highness would *grant me the favor*..."
> (stops writing)

There. Much better. For a start.

SEBASTIAN
You acquired all your elegance and charm at Leopold's court.

ANNA
No, that's where I learned how to survive using it. Those were marvelous days, but there were wolves amongst the sheep. I had to keep my wits about me.

SEBASTIAN
And what shapely wits.

ANNA
(indicating harpsichord)
Play.

SEBASTIAN
(plays a moment, writes on the manuscript, then stops)
His Highness Frederick Augustus II reminds me of Leopold in his favor of my music.

ANNA
(reading, then commenting)
Another clumsy remark. You need to make your points with charm and panache.

SEBASTIAN
Write charm and panache into it, then. I have no time for it.
(ANNA continues reading letter and SEBASTIAN goes back to the Kyrie. ANNA is writing something, then stops)

ANNA
I hope Friede doesn't get lonely in Dresden.

SEBASTIAN
He isn't there yet. He has first to win the position.

ANNA
He already loves the city. They will easily fall in love with him.

(SEBASTIAN stops playing and is making notation on the manuscript)

SEBASTIAN
I heard someone say Leipzig is "A city of baboons with beards and skirts." He will do well to leave now. He doesn't belong here.

ANNA
And what about you? Do you belong here? Why is it only monarchs appreciate you?

SEBASTIAN
God's will.

ANNA
If this is His will, then He is a cruel God! One who ignites a passion and a fire of extraordinary abilities in a man, only to quench it every time it flames with power. Why give that fire at all? Does He laugh at you, for your feeble efforts?

SEBASTIAN
More likely cries. My passion, my fire, as you call it, is the very fabric of eternity we begin weaving here, in this life, on earth. It comes with a price.

ANNA
Then clearly the price is too high.

SEBASTIAN
It isn't for me. I pay it willingly.

ANNA
Then you are alone! God be merciful, but I reject it all. I would rather have one moment of *your* cool, sweet passion, than one hundred of God's all consuming fires!

> (ANNA leaves letter, and exits, angrily. FRIEDE enters, passing her by)

FRIEDE
I see your charm has won her over once more.

SEBASTIAN
I don't wish to hurt her. One day she will understand.

FRIEDE
I doubt it. *I* don't.

SEBASTIAN
But you do. Where I won't dare, you stare, hard, and unblinking, deep into the abyss.

FRIEDE
Thank you for that negative compliment.

SEBASTIAN
No, you don't see. I mean that you are strong. You have something of a reckless courage, but it makes you stand where others shrink.

FRIEDE
Against exactly that you have always fought me. Why this, now?

SEBASTIAN
Enough of this sentimental foolery. Let's get on with your audition piece. Play.
> (FRIEDE sits the harpsichord and plays Prelude and Fugue in G major BWV 541. FRIEDE plays it quite fast, but accurately. SEBASTIAN paces room, lights his pipe. He's having trouble lighting it. He gets it lit, then turns and with a rather impish look, takes off his shoe, and throws it at FRIEDE. FRIEDE stops paying, stunned at being struck by a shoe. He turns and looks hard at his father, sees his father's impish smile, then laughs)

FRIEDE
I knew your compliments of me would be short-lived!

SEBASTIAN
That WAS a compliment. Now play it without running through it like a chicken coop and you're trying to catch dinner.
> (FRIEDE starts piece over, less rushed, with more feeling, as evidenced in his expression. SEBASTIAN retrieves his shoe, holds it, pacing with one shoe on and one off, smoking his pipe, and listening. Lights down)

ACT 2 SCENE 6

(September, 1733. Bach home. ANNA is copying out music for SEBASTIAN, while he is putting together some papers into a satchel for travel)

ANNA
(pointing to several pages of music)
Why? S. D. G. Soli Deo Gloria on *every* work?
(SEBASTIAN takes a look at the page, ANNA point and reads)
Why not to God *and* Johann Sebastian Bach be the glory?
(SEBASTIAN doesn't answer but goes back to what he was doing)
"My sins afflict me, like pus in my bones." I remember these words. I sang them long ago. "Puss" and "mire." Appropriate.

SEBASTIAN
(takes one manuscript page)
Wait. Look here. I have written something even more appropriate.
(points to the manuscript page, showing her, but she won't look at it)
Here. P.T.M.N.

ANNA
Which stands for...?

SEBASTIAN
Please. Take. Me. Now!

ANNA
It isn't fair. None of it. It never ends with you.
(SEBASTIAN takes ANNA into his arms. FRIEDE has begun to enter the room, but seeing them, he has fallen back, unseen, but we can see him)

SEBASTIAN
Let me drag all thoughts of puss and mire out of your mind. You know I know how.

ANNA
Yes, you do...and I would be gladly dragged, but...

(SEBASTIAN stops her by kissing her. She releases herself as they see FRIEDE)

                    SEBASTIAN
Friede. I know, yes. We're late.
          (to ANNA)
Let's pick up where we left off when I get back.

                    ANNA
I doubt it!

                    SEBASTIAN
Where are the copies of the Missa?

                    ANNA
In the desk.

                    SEBASTIAN
When is the carriage coming?

                    FRIEDE
At noon.

                    SEBASTIAN
I'll meet you outside. Be sure you have everything.
          (SEBASTIAN exits. FRIEDE stands, almost transfixed. Silence)

                    ANNA
I just want to say how happy I am for you.

                    FRIEDE
Dresden wishes to add a modern Bach. Apparently, I fit the bill.

                    ANNA
That is a good thing.

                    FRIEDE
Yes, my being out of here will be.

                    ANNA
I didn't mean…

FRIEDE

Well, it doesn't matter now. In his mind I'm already gone. No great loss. To him, I am just another player who cannot compose.

ANNA

That's not true. He's always encouraged your compositions.

FRIEDE

He said, quote..."Well Friede, let's get you a position you can hang onto with your kind of talent." Hang on to with my kind of talent? Like a court jester? A trained monkey.

ANNA

You're so wrong. Look at how he has worked with you to get this position.

FRIEDE

As a mere player, while he's applied for the King's Court Capelle position. Don't you see how he degrades and mocks me with this?

ANNA

At Dresden you will be respected for *all* your talents. Except they *may* laugh at how you wear your coat. Still a boy when it comes to dressing. Let me fix this.
    (fixing the collar on his coat)
There. I will miss you, my Ruggerio.

FRIEDE

And you, my Angelica. I'm so lonely already.
    (FRIEDE goes to ANNA and embraces her. She embraces him, to comfort him)

ANNA

You'll be alright. We'll visit you.
    (He starts to kiss her. His kissing becomes more and more passionate. ANNA tries to pull away, but not violently)
Please, don't. I know...I know...But you have to...stop. Friede.
    (SEBASTIAN calls from the other room)

SEBASTIAN
Anna, are all the parts to the Missa in...
> (They have not heard him. He enters, watches for a moment, is stunned, then bellows)

I see...
> (FRIEDE, on hearing him, stops suddenly. SEBASTIAN speaks more softly)

I see my son has continued to become unusually attached to his adopted mother.

ANNA
Don't...

SEBASTIAN
Your passion should be reserved for your music.

FRIEDE
My music? What do you care about my music?

ANNA
Sebastian, just leave him.

FRIEDE
It will take more than a well-aimed shoe, now, won't it? It doesn't matter. I'll soon be far from here. You have made that possible by securing my trained monkey position.

SEBASTIAN
I have had enough!

FRIEDE
Had enough of my reckless courage?
> (FRIEDE is ready for a blow. SEBASTIAN goes to him and looks as if he would strike him, but then puts his arm down, and turns to leave. He takes the satchel, moves to the door, and stops)

SEBASTIAN
I am going to the carriage. Once we are in Dresden, I will try to forget what has happened here.

FRIEDE
I will never forget it.

(ANNA goes to SEBASTIAN, but he wards her off)

SEBASTIAN
Leave it alone. No more talk. It's between us now.

(SEBASTIAN exits. FRIEDE starts to leave. ANNA goes to touch his arm, but he shrugs her off him and leaves without looking back at her. ANNA picks up one page of the manuscript on the table, and then puts it down, speaking without reading anything)

ANNA
"Dearest God, Have mercy on me. Grant me solace and grace. Help me, Jesus, Lamb of God. I am sinking deep in mire."

(Lights down)

ACT 2 SCENE 7

(Summer 1738. Choir loft of St. Thomas. SEBASTIAN and KREBS are in the choir loft. KREBS stands quietly, nervously, as SEBASTIAN questions him. TWO WOMEN are silently at prayer, below, in the church)

SEBASTIAN
And they are all following his orders?

KREBS
That's what they all said.

SEBASTIAN
Insolent, indecent hooligans.

KREBS
Herr Rector Ernesti said he will suspend all the singing money of the choirboys if they don't recognize him as the new appointed Prefect. They have been given strict orders not to sing under anyone but him. They are to come at 1:00. He should be here soon.

SEBASTIAN
What about Kittler?

KREBS
He has given in, too. He will do whatever Herr Rector says.

SEBASTIAN
I should have guessed it. Then why are *you* here, now, with me?

KREBS
(smiles)
I am not fond of Herr Rector Ernesti. I am using this as a way to demonstrate it.

SEBASTIAN
This could get you expelled.

KREBS
Then so be it, if it be God's will.

SEBASTIAN
(going to KREBS and patting him on the shoulder)
There's an honest and good man. Do you think he *will* show up? Our "Prefect?"

KREBS
If Herr Rector requires it, he will obey.

SEBASTIAN
What a dilemma of names! Herr Ernesti drives out my good man, Krause, to put in his incompetent Krause. Then they have the gall to threaten my good Krause with a thrashing for obeying me. Tortured like that, and for what? He had to run away. All designed to humiliate me. All designed for folly.
(rather loudly)
Dumb sheep! Mule! Witless, mindless, incompetent…
(He stops as he sees the TWO WOMEN below, in the church, at prayer, stop and look up. SEBASTIAN looks down and nods to them, and smiles. They go on with their praying. As they do, JG KRAUSE enters, and makes his way up to the choir loft. He sees SEBASTIAN half-way up. He steels himself, and continues up, passes him by and puts down a satchel, opens it and busies himself in it without saying a word. SEBASTIAN quotes Proverbs 26:11)
"As a dog returns to his vomit, so a fool returns to his folly."
(JG KRAUSE looks up momentarily, then continues silently through his papers. He pulls out a certain manuscript, and places it out so he can see it)
Johann Gottlieb Krause.

JG KRAUSE
(without looking up, still busying himself with the music)
Yes, Kapellmeister.

SEBASTIAN
Will you not look me in the eye when I address you?

JG KRAUSE
(without looking up)
No, Kapellmeister.

SEBASTIAN
Why?

JG KRAUSE
I have been instructed not to speak to you, Kapellmeister.

SEBASTIAN
By whom?

JG KRAUSE
I don't wish to cause any problems. I just...

SEBASTIAN
(bellows)
Who?!

JG KRAUSE
Herr Rector Ernesti, Kapellmeister!
(SEBASTIAN goes to him and rips the manuscript papers from his hands. JG KRAUSE takes a step back, then looks as if he is trying to defend himself from a blow. SEBASTIAN just stands there looking at him, then looks at the music)

SEBASTIAN
(examining the music, having a hard time seeing it)
Vespers.
(thinking)
Krebs? Krebs??
(KREBS, who had retreated to one side, moves into the light and is finally noticed by JG KRAUSE, who gives him a little bit of a look of wonder)

KREBS
Yes, Kapellmeister?

SEBASTIAN
(handing him the music)
You conduct this.

KREBS
I...I would be most honored, Kapellmeister.

(at this JG KRAUSE becomes riled, and tries to control his contempt)

JG KRAUSE

I was instructed not to speak to you, Kapellmeister, unless absolutely necessary. I believe now I must. According to the rules set forth in the school laws, it is not for you to appoint the Prefect, but for the Superintendent to choose and *overrule* the Cantor's choice, if he deems it is necessary, so as not to undermine and seriously weaken the morale of the choir.

SEBASTIAN
(unable to believe his ears, full of rage)

What?

JG KRAUSE

And if I were to find you here when I arrived, I was told to...*demand* that you leave the loft and take up your case with Herr Rector.
> (SEBASTIAN is beside himself with rage. He takes any music that he sees and flings it at JG KRAUSE, who is shocked and frightened)

SEBASTIAN

How dare you, you witless, mindless hound, who follows only his master's will and has none for himself! Spineless...dissolute dog!
> (SEBASTIAN chases JG KRAUSE around the choir loft, taking off his shoe and his wig and flinging them at him as he speaks)

You tell your dog master, your Herr Rector, that he had better not continue to interfere with me, or I will feed you, his precious hound, to the hell jackals from whence you came. And if he wishes to malign my character by attempting to humiliate me in the face of the choirboys, and prejudice them against me and impede my duties, he will have to send better than you, his whining infant, to take over my office.
> (stops chasing him)

He must instruct the student-body to show me the respect and obedience due me! Do you hear what I have said?

JG KRAUSE

The whole church hears you, Kapellmeister!

SEBASTIAN
(throwing things at him violently)

Then run! Run back to your master! Go tell him, you drooling beast!
> (JG KRAUSE has run down the stairs, as SEBASTIAN has flung the last object at him. The TWO WOMEN are indignant, and exit as JG KRAUSE exits. KREBS takes a step toward SEBASTIAN, and is about to speak, but then changes his mind and starts to leave)

Krebs!
> (KREBS stops and turns, a little frightened. SEBASTIAN speaks kindly)

I thank you. You are both a gifted student...and a faithful man.

KREBS
I am honored that you think it, Kapellmeister.

SEBASTIAN
Go home before they find you here with me. No use being expelled for a lost battle.

KREBS
Lost? No...I....thank you.
> (KREBS does a deep bow, then leaves the choir loft quickly, and as he gets to the bottom go the stairs, sees SCHEIBE in the shadows. KREBS stops, looking at him questioningly, confused. SCHEIBE gives him a nod of the head, and KREBS returns it, then turns and leaves. SEBASTIAN is collecting all the music and objects he tossed at JG KRUASE as he ran down the stairs form the choir loft, when he sees SCHEIBE standing off to one side)

SEBASTIAN
Herr Scheibe. Hiding in the shadows? What a pleasant surprise. I pray you were here for the show. Were you taking it all down?

SCHEIBE
Enough to fill a volume.

SEBASTIAN
The Passions of Kapellmeister Bach, unabridged.

SCHEIBE
He deserved it.

SEBASTIAN
From your mouth to Herr Ernesti's ears. Actually, I am naturally more a man of peace.

SCHEIBE
I find that hard to believe after what I have just seen.

SEBASTIAN
There are times to be gentle as a dove, and other times, it is best to be wise as a serpent. Which always involves a well-aimed strike, with or without the venom. I used my best fang, but tried not to make it too deadly. Do you think I succeeded?

SCHEIBE
I am sure before the day's end you will need another well-aimed strike.

SEBASTIAN
With or without venom? I am sure you didn't come to hear me reprimand miscreants.

SCHEIBE
I thought I might find you here, rehearsing.

SEBASTIAN
For a war, yes, I suppose I am rehearsing for war. So many wars. Always an enemy.

> (SEBASTIAN collects things he tossed. SCHEIBE follows him as he talks)

SCHEIBE
I have wanted to meet with you. I suppose I should be flattered that you consider me important enough to attack, but I wish it wasn't being done so underhandedly.

SEBASTIAN
I have done nothing underhandedly. I have made my views of your attacks quite clear.

SCHEIBE
I don't see them as clear. But what you call *my* attack, I hope you will see as my sincere wish to...
    (handing SEBASTIAN the object he found)
...enlighten you.

SEBASTIAN
I am beginning to hate that word.

SCHEIBE
There is no reason to continue this fight in such vague terms. I demand that you publically debate me on this subject.

SEBASTIAN
Demand? I don't want to fight you. I am tired of fighting.

SCHEIBE
It is not a fight. It is a debate.

SEBASTIAN
Mud flinging; only in this case, it is using words. I won't lower myself to such things.

SCHEIBE
I resent that you won't publically debate me so I may defend my case.

SEBASTIAN
I have nothing to say that I haven't already said quite clearly in my music.

SCHEIBE
I hardly consider a Dramma per Musica a comprehensive statement of your position.

SEBASTIAN
Those who have heard *The Contest Between Phoebus and Pan* would beg to differ. They have applauded the artful way I have made my argument simple, to the point, and powerfully entertaining. This I have heard from both nobleman and merchant.

SCHEIBE
I think you are afraid.

SEBASTIAN
Afraid? What? Of you?

SCHEIBE
No. The new music.

SEBASTIAN
I have never been afraid of any music.

SCHEIBE
Then I challenge you to write in this style.

SEBASTIAN
No.

SCHEIBE
Why? Is it beneath you?

SEBASTIAN
No.

SCHEIBE
Surely it is not too difficult for you.

SEBASTIAN
The Collegium Musicum will perform *Phoebus and Pan* at Zimmermann's Coffee House within the month. On this subject, I will speak through that alone.
    (moves close to SCHEIBE)
You have to understand...I am not my own man. I am like the bush set before Moses. Burning, but never consumed. Melted down, yet will the Refiner see a perfect imagine of Himself in me? Still too much dross. I will continue to burn, until He, and only HE, puts another tune in me.

SCHEIBE
God's music, then? Is ours merely man's? What a notion! So you choose to darken your life as a martyr and let go of the world's rich music as it shines brightly in all its *natural* glory? I am sorry for you.

SEBASTIAN
"Full fathom five thy father lies; Of his bones are coral made; Those are pearls that were his eyes: Nothing of him that doth fade, But doth suffer a sea-change, Into something rich and strange."

SCHEIBE
A peculiar saying.

SEBASTIAN
William Shakespeare of England. From a play called the *Tempest*. His corral bones are untouched, immovable, yet…a sea-change. Rich and strange.
   (thinks, as if considering)
No. There is nothing "rich" and "strange" in this new music. Nothing.

   (SEBASTIAN leaves as SCHEIBE stands a moment, as if he would say something. But he shakes his head in pity and leaves. Lights down)

ACT 2 SCENE 8

> (May 7, 1747. The Court of Frederick the Great at Potsdam. FREDERICK is not dressed in kingly robes, but royal clothing befitting a man of high office. At court is OLD MUSICIAN JONAS, an OFFICER, CPE and FREDERICK, who stands with music in his hand, and a flute in the other. He looks over the music with OLD MUSICIAN JONAS)

OLD MUSICIAN JONAS
I will pay the Viola de Gamba and Carl Philipp Emmanuel will play one of your fortepianos, if you wish, Your Highness.

FREDERICK
I would rather you played the harpsichord for this.

CPE
Yes, Your Highness.
> (the OFFICER enters, and bows, handing FREDERICK a piece of paper)

OFFICER
The list, Your Highness. You will see he has only just arrived this evening, with his son. They are close by.

> (FREDERICK looks over the list, and then to OFFICER and OLD MUSICIAN JONAS)

FREDERICK
So, gentlemen, Old Bach is come. Go. Fetch him immediately.
> (OFFICER bows and leaves)

I have waited all my life to meet a man of genius. I believe this is the time.

OLD MUSICIAN JONAS
> (to CPE)

There are all sorts of mighty kings with mighty purposes that serve in the world. Before us is one...
> (bows to FREDERICK)

And Old Bach, your father, is another. May his reign be as gloriously proclaimed as any emperor's.

FREDERICK
You speak like a philosopher and not a musician, Jonas.

OLD MUSICIAN JONAS
I humbly beg your pardon.

FREDERICK
No need. I am sure you are correct.

OLD MUSICIAN JONAS
(to CPE)
I was fortunate to hear your father play in Dresden in 1717, when a competition was held between him and the famous Louis Marchand, organist to Louis XV of France. The concertmaster, old Volumier, had a grudge against him and suggested it. He knew your father could play rings around Marchand. I was among the large company of persons of high rank come to watch. But when it came time for the concert, Marchand was gone. Rumor had it he had heard your father play and ran off like a frightened rabbit. Your father played a solo concert and I have never heard such sublime sounds on any instrument since. Excepting, of course, the strains of His Highness's flute.

FREDERICK
Of course, my dear Old Jonas.

(OFFICER enters, followed by SEBASTIAN and FREIDE. They are both in traveling clothes. OFFICER announces them)

OFFICER
Herr Bach and son, Wilhelm Friedemann Bach. His Majesty, Frederick II, King of Prussia.

(SEBASTIAN and FRIEDE enter, bowing, and FREDERICK nods)

FREDERICK
Welcome. Now embrace your son, Old Bach! You have a grandchild by him.

(SEBASTIAN embraces CPE heartily and FREIDE embraces him as well)

SEBASTIAN
Thank you, Your Highness. I am looking forward to seeing the child. I am sorry I was not able to change into a proper Cantor's robe.

FREDERICK
Traveling clothes befits you, Kapellmeister. I prefer my comfort to kingly robes, as you can see.

SEBASTIAN
Here is Carl Philipp Emmanuel's older brother, Wilhelm Friedemann.

FRIEDE
(bowing low)
Your Highness.

FREDERICK
Yes. Enough of these formalities. They bore me. I have a great adventure designed for this evening. I would have played my Pan pipe as usual, but your arrival has changed everything, and I am delighted. First, come, have some coffee with me.

SEBASTIAN
I would very pleased, Your Highness.

FREDERICK
(to OFFICER)
Bring some.
(OFFICER exits)
I prefer it boiled in champagne. Both are French and belong together. Then we will see the fortepianos. I want your opinion. These are the new versions of what you saw once before, when you voiced your mind about them being too soft at the top. Yes, these have been manufactured by, Herr Gottfried Silbermann, a true master in such arts.

SEBASTIAN
He is a marvel.

FREDERICK
You will see they are all beauties to behold. All works of fine craftsmanship, and superb art. But will they sing in the high notes as in the low?

SEBASTIAN
I am sure of it. Will you learn to play the fortepiano, Your Highness?

FREDERICK
Me? Oh, no. The flute is my only toy. Your son, Carl Philipp Emmanuel, will continue to play on them.

SEBASTIAN
Then he has already tested them for Your Highness?

FREDERICK
Yes.

SEBASTIAN
And do they sing?

CPE
Under my fingers they are pet canaries, in comparison to my father, who will make them sing as larks and nightingales.

FREDERICK
I see. Then it is your father I should hire for my court clavier player.

SEBASTIAN
Carl Philipp Emmanuel will amaze you, I am sure, on any clavier. I pray that these fine instruments will sing for you for many years to come, and not lose their strong voice.

FREDERICK
They will be played and played, day and night.

OLD MUSICIAN JONAS
(aside, quietly, to SEBASTIAN & FRIEDE)
Until he tires of them and they sit in corners, untouched.

FREDERICK
Tomorrow you will play all the organs in the whole city of Potsdam. I want to hear you make them sing, too.

SEBASTIAN
I am looking forward to the concerts, Your Highness.

OLD MUSICIAN JONAS
(aside, quietly to SEBASTIAN & FRIEDE)
They are in the churches. They will fare better.

FREDERICK
Jonas? Go and bring in the mahogany. I want to hear that first.
(OLD MUSICIAN JONAS exits)
He thinks I don't notice him jabbering in whispers about my extravagance with these new instruments. He is like an old uncle. If I was my father's son I would have had him flogged for insolence. But I am a civil despot. Very...French.
(lightly)
Well, now. I wish to hear all the Bachs play today. Sons *and* father. Sons are such delights, are they not, Old Bach?

SEBASTIAN
Yes.

FREDERICK
Then I would like to hear Wilhelm Friedemann play first.

SEBASTIAN
Why not Carl Philipp Emmanuel?

FREDERICK
I wanted to hear his compositions. He has charmed all Dresden with them.

SEBASTIAN
But as you know, Your Highness, Carl also has many...

FREDERICK
But I have heard his compositions for seven years. He is my own court harpsichordist and can play for me any time.

SEBASTIAN
Friedemann is likely worn out from the journey, and would not be up to his usual...

FREDERICK
He looks quite capable to me. Wilhelm Friedemann will play first. I insist.

SEBASTIAN
With all due respect, Your Highness...

FRIEDE
(cutting SEBASTIAN off)
His Highness wishes to hear one of my compositions, and you have taught me, Father, to humbly respect the desires of any authority above and beyond my own, have you not? Then I *humbly* submit to His Highness, no matter how wretched I may feel at this moment.

(SEBASTIAN is stunned and speak right away. He faces FREDERICK)

SEBASTIAN
As Your Highness wishes.

FREDERICK
(to FRIEDE)
Have I your permission, then?

FRIEDE
Of course, Your Highness.

FREDERICK
This doesn't go against any wishes of your own to please your father?

FRIEDE
My father and I...we rarely see eye to eye. I am too much the wild artist and not enough the craftsman.

FREDERICK
But you have inherited great talents from your father.

FRIEDE
In music, yes. But in others, I am afraid I fall sadly short.

SEBASTIAN
I am incredibly proud of *both* my sons...Your Highness.

FREDERICK

I see.
    (pauses, then goes to his flute)
It is hard when the man issued from your own flesh is not like you. It makes one angry, I think.
    (takes his flute in his hands and plays a few notes, then)
My father showed his anger about it by beating me in public to humiliate me. To show his displeasure with his "philosopher" son. I foolishly tried to escape. Run away with my dear...*only* friend, Katte. But he caught us. He decided this was a perfect opportunity to toughen me into his soldier.
    (pause)
He had Katte beheaded and forced me to watch. The brutality of it nearly killed me.
    (plays a few notes on the flute, then lighter)
As a result, I have grown. I am very much an "Enlightened Despot." I have understood pain. How to inflict it and how to recover after merciless blows. However...the son never became the father.
    (speaks in French)
"Le dessein de Dieu comprend à la fois des colombes et des serpents."
    (Friede and CPE understand, but Sebastian doesn't. Friede is not willing to translate it, and is a little rattled by it, and CPE is embarrassed, so Frederick translates it)
"God's design includes both doves and serpents." But who is who? C'est la vie.
    (smiles)
It is only a clumsy observation on my part. Pay it no mind.
    (taking Sebastian by the shoulder)
Come, my "Old Bach" and play for me on my fortepianos. Or is it pianofortes? What are they being called these days? I must know.
    (OFFICER arrives carrying a tray with delicate coffee cups)
Magnifique! Indulge with me.
    (FREDERICK takes one coffee cup and hands it to SEBASTIAN. CPE and FRIEDE take their cups, as the OFFICER leaves with the tray)

SEBASTIAN

Nectar of the gods.

                    FREDERICK

Wonderful! Nectar of the gods.
   (holds up his own cup)
A toast to all of us gods.
   (ALL take a cup and hold it up for the toast, then drink. Lights
   are dimmed. During this section there are many harpsichord
   pieces played which blend one into the other. It is a
   kaleidoscope of sounds, one following the other. It is mainly the
   Goldberg Variations and moving into a mix of The Musical
   Offering. The action takes place in the dim light. We see OLD
   MUSICIAN JONAS wheel in the fortepiano to a particular spot.
   FRIEDE is indicated by FREDERICK to sit and play. FRIEDE
   does, and we see FREDERICK watching SEBASTIAN more closely
   than looking at FRIEDE to observe his reaction. FRIEDE plays
   the Goldberg Variation, Aria 2, finishes and there is polite
   applause by ALL. FREDERICK indicates that SEBASTIAN should
   now go and play, so he puts down his coffee cup and sits in a
   chair at the instrument.   OFFICER returns with a large tray with
   royal-looking, delicate coffee cups and a coffee container,
   looking like a glorified teapot, all of which is placed to one side,
   and he exits. FREIDE gets another cup. SEBASTIAN continues
   playing. The passage of time is indicated by the OFFICER
   returning with a candelabra, to place on the fortepiano, as it is
   getting darker and darker. The main light now seems to be from
   this candelabra. CPE, holding his coffee cup, is still standing
   very close to the fortepiano, just beyond FREDERICK, who is
   enraptured by SEBASTIAN'S playing. FREIDE returns to where
   he was seated, off to one side, seeming to be both tired and
   frustrated. SEBASTIAN ends the fugue and FREDERICK claps
   enthusiastically. SEBASTIAN rises from the fortepiano's seat,
   bows graciously)

                    FREDERICK
That was sublime. An improvisation of immense perplexity. I marvel
at the ease in which you produce such works with no letting up. That
a mere man can do all this.

                    SEBASTIAN
God's gift. Playing beautiful music on any instrument is no great
mystery. All you have to do is touch the right key at the right time and
the instrument will play itself.

FREDERICK
God's gift, indeed. Now, how many has that been?

CPE
I would count this as number fifteen, Your Highness.

SEBSASTIAN
Sixteen. A Gigue, allemande, gavotte, two minuets, no three.

CPE
The French courrant. An Italian corrente.

SEBASTIAN
Three canons and five fugues. I have now finished the circular trip through all the rooms and I am back at this one, where I began.

CPE
No, it is seventeen. You are forgetting the riddle cannon.

FREDERICK
I would never have guessed it was in the length of the notes. Long-lived notes, like, "Long live the king!" Carl Philipp Emmanuel was so quick witted about it. I will have to spend more time on such things if I am to compete with him solving them.

CPE
Please, Your Highness, there is no competition.

FREDERICK
Isn't there? War? Sex? Hunger? Life is wrought with the hell of them, isn't it? But look, here, Old Bach. I have an idea. I want an even more complex piece than one of your canon riddles. I want a fugue with six obbligato parts.

SEBASTIAN
Alright. Then you supply the melody for the subject.

FREDERICK
Splendid! I have just the one. I was about to perform it this evening. Here.
   (goes to get the music, and bring sit back)
This. I love it. Play.

(SEBASTIAN plays it, then stops and plays it again)

SEBASTIAN
It is beautiful, but it won't do for a six part obbligato. For three, it would be perfect.

FREDERICK
Then make it three. God's number. The perfect number. Go ahead and create a holy trinity of sound for me!
> (SEBASTIAN plays a fugue using the melody as the subject and creates, apparently on the spot, a fugue of great complexity. OLD MUSICIAN JONAS returns, OFFICER, and TWO WOMAN of the court enter, slowly and gather around the fortepiano, but at a slight distance, looking quite taken and amazed at what they are hearing. SEBASTIAN plays on and on, with this fugue flowing into one with 6 obbligato parts. The music will all be from the soon to be composed *Musical Offering*. As SEBASTIAN plays, FREDERICK plays some notes on his flute, and then exclaims loudly, seeming rather overly happy, so probably a little drunk)

Play, Old Bach! Through the night. And in the morning we shall watch the heavens open up its great door. And like Venus, you will rise, the new morning star, above it all, outshining every living thing. Play. Et permettez-moi de mourir dans les bras de la musique tels du ciel.

> (The translation of French – "And may I die in the arms of such music from heaven." FREDERICK conducts at a distance while SEBASTIAN plays and ALL gather closer around the fortepiano, with CPE. FRIEDE remains alone and aloof, seated where he has been. Lights down slowly)

ACT 2 SCENE 9

(Late December, 1749. Bach home. There is a small cage with a small bird, a linnet, which is a songbird, inside. ANNA looks at it with admiration)

ANNA
She's lovely. I don't want to know the cost. I am sure it was extravagant.

SEBASTIAN
Let's just say, my drinking of ale through the Christmas season will be rather light. Several kegs lighter.

ANNA
See? You shouldn't have.
 (smiles coyly)
But I am so glad you did. I don't think a more lovely thing could be given to a songbird...than a songbird. Will she sing?

SEBASTIAN
She sang beautifully for a nobleman. I know she will sing even more heroically for you.

ANNA
Don't use the word "hero." It conjures up things I don't wish to think of now.

SEBASTIAN
 (does a gallant stance, taking his arm up, as if to wield a sword)
Not too old for a gallant rescue of a maiden in distress from her enemies? Or is my weariness showing through my shiny knight's armor?

ANNA
Yes. *Your* enemies. That's what I need to be saved from. The endless parade of them all lined up at our door, each waiting their turn for a bite. Why do you enrage so many?

SEBASTIAN
Is the question how many enemies can I fight at once? Let's see. Herr Scheibe? The council? The students? Friede? There is a dark alley with no hope. And now you? Why not top it off with your contempt for me as a failure.

ANNA
I never said you were a failure.

SEBASTIAN
You don't have to. I have to come to terms with it myself. This is the last painful twist of that thorn in my flesh. When it is done, I will either run, or finally accept it.

ANNA
Accept what? Defeat? You are a pillar of strength.

SEBASTIAN
Strength? I used to be strong. But I am tired of the fight. Now I want to give up. There is no comfort in any of this.

ANNA
I used to be a comfort to you.

SEBASTIAN
I am blind to all comfort. I am falling into an abyss. The world is filled with deep shadows with no definition. All forms are unrecognizable. Even you. I am so tired,

ANNA
How dare you surrender to this! Failure and falling, with no hope. I won't listen!
    (ANNA cups her hands over her ears and starts to sing "A Mighty Fortress is Our God" in German)

SEBASTIAN
Anna. Anna, stop acting like you're…You're acting like an infant. And a spoiled one.
    (ANNA continues as same)
Anna Magdalena Wülken!
    (ANNA stops singing, opens her eyes, and looks at SEBASTIAN)

ANNA
What did you call me?

SEBASTIAN
Anna Magdalena Wülken.

ANNA
Why did you call me by my family name and not my marriage name?

SEBASTIAN
Because...I felt the need to...to court you again.

ANNA
Court me? What on earth...?

SEBASTIAN
I wanted to start over. As if we had never met. Full of promise. I am now seeing you for the first time and I am immediately falling in love with you. But I have to catch your attention somehow, because you will certainly be paying me no mind. Who am I to an attractive, vivacious and talented woman of your caliber? And so wickedly beautiful.

ANNA
I don't like your word choice there.

SEBASTIAN
Angelically beautiful.

ANNA
I don't think I can play this game, Sebastian.

SEBASTIAN
It's no game. I am falling, it is true. But instead of into the abyss, I am leaning your way. May I fall into your arms, instead?

ANNA
Now you are being silly.
    (SEBASTIAN starts to sway, as if he would faint)

SEBASTIAN
Why is it so warm? The pain. It's like a fire stabbing inside my head.
>(he almost falls, as ANNA helps him to a chair)

Where are you?

ANNA
Here, my beloved.

SEBASTIAN
I can't see you.
>(ANNA comes around and kneels down in front of him)

ANNA
Here. Take my hand.
>(ANNA holds out her hand for him to take, but he is having trouble seeing it)

SEBASTIAN
>(he is having trouble forming the words)

W-where? I c-can't...see you...
>(he suddenly holds his head and falls over, off the chair, onto the floor, fainted)

ANNA
Sebastian!
>(goes to him and tries to revive him, but he doesn't come to)

Oh, God! What's happened?
>(ANNA remains on the floor with SEBASTIAN)

Don't die on me, Johann Sebastian Bach! Not yet! Not now!

>(ANNA holds SEBSASTIAN'S head in her lap and strokes it. Lights down)

ACT 2 SCENE 10

(Early January, 1750. One week after stroke. SEBASTIAN is seated, alone, with a lap blanket and his Calov bible, in the comfortable chair. He is trying to read, holding bible in various positions. He rubs his eyes and head. He tries again, but can't. Tries to rise, but finds he is weakened. He nearly swoons, tries to stop himself from falling, and in the process, flings the blanket and bible far from him. He manages to sit down again, but is now very frustrated and is trying to reach for both. While he tries, ANNA enters, carrying a tray of food, placing it on the table. He immediately stops and acts as if he is asleep. ANNA sees the blanket bible on the floor, looks a little puzzled, then bemused)

ANNA
You can cut out the fake snoring.

SEBASTIAN
Huh? What? What, Anna?

ANNA
I can see the Bible and blanket have spontaneously exploded off your lap and ended up way over there. Wouldn't be that you tried to get up again, would it?

SEBASTIAN
No, no. Just dozed off. They must've...fallen.
    (ANNA gives him a look, as she prepares the food on the tray)
I know. I have never been a convincing liar. But I can't read here.

ANNA
Then I'll bring you another lamp.

SEBASTIAN
No. It isn't the light. It is something else. There is a cloud cover, like a storm, over my eyes and in my head. I can't concentrate. The pain.

ANNA
The doctor said inflamed eyes can be very painful.
    (brings SEBASTIAN food tray. Retrieves blanket and Bible and puts them aside)

SEBASTIAN
(examining the food)
What is this? I can't make it out. Is it beef? By the smell, it is. Is it cut? I can't...see...
(picks up a utensil and tries to use it but it falls to the floor)

ANNA
Oh, Sebastian.
(goes to him, takes his hand, trying not to let her emotions get the best of her)
Here. I'll do it.

SEBASTIAN
(pushes her away)
No.
(tries again, but misses plate, knocking some food to ground. He throws utensil. ANNA takes his hand, kisses it, then kneels at his feet and cuts his meat)

ANNA
You rest.

SEBASTIAN
I can't have you do this. I am not an infant.

ANNA
That may be so, but if you are good boy, I might let you suckle at my breast.
(SEBASTIAN smiles and strokes her head as she continues cutting)
And no more sneaking ale until you're better. And no pipe smoking.

SEBASTIAN
This is turning into a purgatory with no heaven in sight.

ANNA
Carl will be coming in a fortnight. Friede is busy in...

SEBASTIAN
No! Nothing of him.

ANNA
That's not fair. He's worried about you.

SEBASTIAN
No, it isn't fair. I am sorry. I can't see through my eyes very well, but my heart has had its eyes pried wide open. I do love him, Anna. But I can't tell him. Not yet.

ANNA
I know.
    (Knock at the door)
The good doctor.
    (ANNA rises, exits to door)

SEBASTIAN
Nothing good about it unless he claims me as cured.
    (ANNA enters with KREBS and he stands before SEBASTIAN)
Is this Krebs?

KREBS
The same, Kapellmeister.

SEBASTIAN
I'm sorry I can't say good to see you, as I can hardly see you, so it is not at all good. Please sit down and have some beef and ale.

KREBS
Thank you, but, please, I will have only the ale.

ANNA
Yes, you may, but Herr Bach may not.
    (SEBASTIAN makes a face. ANNA exits)

KREBS
You look well.

SEBASTIAN
You are a worse liar than I am!

KREBS
They are worried about you at the school. Anxious for your return.

SEBASTIAN
Another lie. They were all watching carefully to see if I would die before the year's end. But I beat them. The doctor said it was a stroke. But we must keep that hidden. So we are speaking only of the eye problem. I have been in correspondence with a London physician who has done many successful eye operations. He calls them "cataract couching." A strange name, but he says I am a good candidate and he will cure me.

KREBS
I am glad.
    (Knock at the door)

SEBASTIAN
Our family doctor. He's expected. Anna! Krebs will get it! Please, do you mind?
    (KREBS answers the door. ANGELINA WOLFF enters, carrying a basket)

ANGELINA
Hello. Are you a son of the Cantor?

KREBS
Oh, no. A student.

SEBASTIAN
Come in. I am over here.
    (ANNA enters with ale for KREBS)

ANGELINA
Good afternoon, Cantor. Mrs. Bach. I have come to….give you this on behalf of those who wish to help you in this time of…great need in your home.
    (hands ANNA the basket with a little curtsey. ANNA takes it with the same)

ANNA
Thank you very kindly. But I'm sorry. I don't know who you are or who this comes from.

ANGELINA
Many pardons! I am Angelina, the daughter of Mrs. Wolff. Of the church council. The council wishes to know...I mean give tidings...I mean *well wishes* for the speedy recovery of the Cantor. He will be returning to St. Thomas...soon?

SEBASTIAN
Within the week.
    (ANNA looks as if she would protest, but says nothing)
And you can report back to your council that their generosity is only exceeded by the expeditious dispatch of such a mercenary as yourself to ascertain the matter at hand with intelligence and insight.

ANGELINA
    (confused, not sure if it is a compliment)
I...yes, thank...I will tell them you are well. Thank you, Cantor. Mrs. Bach.
    (curtseys and exits)

SEBASTIAN
A spy. I knew they would be sending one, but sending such an innocent as that is cruel.

KREBS
They have gone farther. They are now taking applications.

ANNA
How dare they?

SEBASTIAN
I am not surprised.

KREBS
I have come here to beg your forgiveness. I have put in one, myself.

SEBASTIAN
I congratulate you! No, go ahead. It is good that you apply. You will do them well, if you can stand it.

KREBS

They will see the folly soon, especially when you know who has been applying. Herr Görner. He isn't content being in competition with your Collegium Musicum all these years with his own little band of merchants, but he has to have your Cantor post, too.

SEBASTIAN

What are you playing for your audition.

KREBS

Something of yours.

SEBASTIAN

You take a great risk. It is the new music they will be looking for. Not mine.

KREBS

I wish to make a point, as I did in the choir loft that day, that I am a man of strong principals and will follow through with conviction no matter what the cost.

SEBASTIAN

Then you shall have whatever you wish of mine to play.

KREBS

I promise I will play it brilliantly.

SEBASTIAN

Come back tomorrow and I will have something ready. You will play it for me and I will be the judge of your brilliance.

KREBS

Yes, of course. Thank you.
>   (KREBS bows low, and turns to leave. ANNA escorts him to the door area. SEBASTIAN tries to eat, but continues to have trouble seeing. They speak out of earshot of SEBASTIAN. KREB watches him, then turns to ANNA)

He's the center of the universe...some universe of great importance, anyway. And yet I don't think he sees himself at all that way.

ANNA

No, he doesn't. But he's the center of mine. And after nearly twenty-seven years of marriage, if I hear his footsteps...my heart *still* races.

> (KREBS kisses ANNA on the cheek. She smiles and gives him a brief hug. KREBS exits. Lights down)

ACT 2 SCENE 11

> (Later in January, 1750. At St. Thomas School. KREBS is seated, waiting. To his surprise, SCHEIBE is the one who enters. KREBS stands)

KREBS
Herr Scheibe. I didn't know the council chose you for my audition. I am honored, sir.

SCHEIBE
We shall see. Please sit.
> (KREBS sits again, and SCHEIBE takes a chair and sits by him)

So. You are "the" Krebs. The one favored by Herr Bach.

KREBS
Favored? Oh, I see. You confuse me with Herr Krause.

SCHEIBE
Ah, yes. Krause. There were two of them.

KREBS
Yes.

SCHEIBE
I remember. And I remember you. In the choir loft that day. You are definitely one of his favorites.

KREBS
I am aware that Herr Bach was pleased with my work.

SCHEIBE
Was? You speak as if he is gone? Have you seen him?

KREBS
He is very much alive. I saw him yesterday. He is aware of my applying for this position.

SCHEIBE
Really? Very gracious of him. Tell me. What is it like to be one of his prized pupils?

KREBS
No different than being any other pupil under him.

SCHEIBE
I doubt it. You see, I was there when he made the fine distinction between his favorites and that other poor soul, Krause, by throwing him out of the gallery loft on his unmusical ear. What a scene. Who is worthy and who is not. Has he taught you to be as proud as he is?

KREBS
Proud? I would never use that word when speaking about Kapellmeister Bach.

SCHEIBE
You give yourself away. We are hiring only a Cantor here, not a Kapellmeister. Then he is a not a god to you? The Greeks have a pantheon full of them. Is he not Zeus and you, Hermes, or Mercury or Apollo?

KREBS
I wouldn't pretend to be an equal with him. He is above me in all disciplines. But he is most certainly only human.

SCHEIBE
Then why do those students he favors venerate him so?

KREBS
Vener...? Herr Scheibe, I can assure you, he wouldn't tolerate one second of that kind of behavior. You don't know him. It has never been about the man. All your work to discredit him and his music has already done its damage.

SCHEIBE
You're mistaken. How can I discredit him or his work? He's merely fallen behind the times with music that is old and out of touch. The wisdom of this age has brought that to light.

KREBS
I can see how this interview is going. How can I ever be considered for this post. I'll leave, so as not to cause any more embarrassment.

SCHEIBE

Oh, stop being such a self-righteous fool, and sit down. Let's commence with the matter at hand.
>   (KREBS returns, hesitates to sit. SCHEIBE points to the chair. KREBS sits)

What are the works you will play?

KREBS

Useless.

SCHEIBE

What?

KREBS

I have brought only Herr Bach's compositions.

SCHEIBE

Of course. Please play me the first.
>   (KREBS hesitates)

You're interested in auditioning for the position, are you not? Then play.
>   (KREBS sighs, then gets up, goes to the harpsichord, sits and plays the Prelude to the Prelude and Fugue in C minor, WTC, Book 1. Soon SHREIBE stops him)

Wait. Let me see that.
>   (KREBS hands him the music. SCHIEBE turns the pages, reading it in his head)

I know this. Play the fugue.
>   (hands music back to KREBS, who plays the fugue. He stops him again)

Yes. Very ambitious. And you are proving to be an excellent musician. You see, can't you, that this is what I meant when I said such compositions are...

KREBS

Useless...

>   (KREBS rises from the harpsichord, taking manuscript)

SCHEIBE
I was going to say, exceedingly beautiful, in a way. But thankfully, it is a dying art.

KREBS
What is rising from its ashes to replace it? Couperin's "Le Rossingnol en Amour?" A nightingale twittering endlessly with notes going nowhere? Fluff and fill, expressing nothing. Music is a sacred art...

SCHEIBE
Oh, my dear Krebs...

KREBS
...and those who create it are performing a sacred task, because it is creative. *You* embrace a style simply because it's modern. Music thought of as little more than a luxury...a distraction after tea. Are you content to bury what speaks of the eternal and replace it with the mundane and fashionable? I am not.

SCHEIBE
I am content to replace superstition with the purity and reason of science.

KREBS
Which is a thin disguise for replacing God with man.

SCHEIBE
Science teaches us we no longer have to live in fear of every thunderstorm or mystery of nature, as if it was being manipulated by the whim of an incomprehensible God. The truth is that nature obeys laws. And those laws are inevitable. Man has reason, which enables him to grasp these laws. Grasp them, Krebs.
    (indicating the manuscript)
This ponderous, heavy, twisting, turning...inverting. How can we comprehend it? What *has* your master taught you?

KREBS
Simply...that God is incomprehensible, as is the heavens, and the mysteries of His universe. And that music created for the glory of God will continue to reflect this.

SCHEIBE

Sad, really. Watching your young mind distorted by old thinking. So much misguided sincerity.

(sits at the harpsichord and plays a run of notes)

It pains me to think that this is all you've come away with after years of study with your beloved Herr Bach. Where is the truth? Can't you see? Here...in Couperin...

(plays part of Couperin's "Le Rossignol en Amour.")

This rhythmic structure speaks of the true patterns of *life*?

(plays a little more, then stops, then plays Rameau's "Indes Galante.")

And in Rameau. Here is stability. A natural gait. Simple, light and fanciful. Alive.

(plays a little more and stops)

KREBS

Is that it? Do you sincerely believe all this?

SCHEIBE

No.

(gets up from the harpsichord)

KREBS

What?

SCHEIBE

(pauses as if considering, then smiles)

It has nothing whatsoever to do with science or nature. That...is a smokescreen. But I thought you'd have guessed it. I'll let you in on a little secret.

(leans in to KREBS)

The truth is...no one wants to hear that music anymore. No one has the palate for it. And frankly, Krebs, no one cares. It's passé. Gone. Out of fashion. It's...*baroque*.

(picks up manuscript and waves it as if evidence in court)

Let it go. Why hang on? It's like a dear, but dead uncle, who should now be respectfully buried before he...begins to stink.

KREBS

Let it be so.
> (prepares to leave)

You champion your new, sentimental fluff, with science and reason propped up as god. As for me? I will march on, willingly, with an art that has been condemned to death... and to some, stinks. But in the end, we shall see which of these will *endure*.
> (moves toward exit)

As for this interview, well, I'm sorry to have wasted your time, Herr Scheibe.

> (KREBS exits, forgetting the music manuscript. After he is gone, SCHEIBE walks back to the harpsichord, looks at it, and plays the first subject of the fugue. He stops playing, shrugs, then walks off carrying the manuscript under his arm, whistling Couperin's "Le Rossignol en Amour." Lights down)

ACT 2 SCENE 12

(March, 1750. Setting of opening scene of Act 1. This is 2 months after SEBASTIAN's stroke and 1 week after his second eye operation. He has spent these two months in total darkness. SEBASTIAN is standing by the table. He looks as he did in the opening scene, in the same clothing, his eyes bandaged. He waits a moment, and then with his arms at his sides, takes several deliberate strides in one direction. He stops, turns aside a little, and is about to take more strides, but stops mid-stride and steps back. He stops and thinks, and then deliberately takes a few strides forward. We can now see he is headed for the harpsichord, but if he keeps moving forward at that pace, he will crash into it. As SEBASTIAN is about to crash, ANNA is entering, carrying a tray with dishes and items to set the table for a meal)

ANNA

Sebastian! Stop!

SEBASTIAN

(still in motion)

Watch!

(He makes it to just before harpsichord, where he stops abruptly, and smiles)

It was an exercise in acoustics. I measured the distance from the chair to the harpsichord by the echoes in the room and I figured out the strides.

(He puts out his hands, feeling for the harpsichord. When he touches it, he moves himself around it, finds the seat and sits)

Don't you dare move this!

ANNA

Not likely.

(SEBASTIAN begins to play Art of Fugue, Contrapunctus 4 – Glenn Gould. ANNA sets the table. SEBASTIAN is playing quite vigorously, and then stops, and holds his head, as if he has had a sudden stabbing pain. He looks dizzy and about to faint off the chair. She sees it, runs to him, helping him from swooning to the floor just in time. He starts to cough violently. ANNA is able to help him to the comfortable chair. She goes to the table and pours him a glass of water, returning with it and table napkin. SEBASTIAN coughs into it. It looks messy and bloody. She hands him the water, but he waves it away. She returns to the table)

SEBASTIAN
If you're not going to give me what I want, don't bother.

ANNA
When Dr. Taylor comes, I'm sure he won't approve of a drunk patient.

SEBASTIAN
If we offer him ale, we'll both be drunk and have a much more merry time of it.

ANNA
Rest. Playing like that rattles you so.

SEBASTIAN
It never did before. I want to finish these. They're pounding in my head, trying to get out. I open the door, but it slams closed. These headaches. I want to finish.
(starts coughing violently again. ANNA looks worried but doesn't show him. FRIEDE enters. He is looking older even than in the scene at Frederick's court)

ANNA
Friede! Friede is back.
(FRIEDE stands by the door, not coming in. He looks at ANNA, questioningly. She shakes her head, as if to say SEBASTIAN is not doing well)

SEBASTIAN
Did you get it?

FRIEDE
It took lying and cheating and stealing, but yes, I got it.

SEBASTIAN
I knew I'd sent the right man for the job.
(FRIEDE goes to him with a pouch, placing it into his hands. SEBASTIAN opens it. It contains pipe tobacco. He sniffs it and smiles)

SEBASTIAN (Cont'd)
Good aroma. Thank God my nose still works.

ANNA
You can't smoke with your lungs in this condition.

SEBASTIAN
Watch me.
    (Pulls out his pipe from his jacket and stuffs tobacco into it)
I was thinking. When Carl comes, we can try the reworked fugues. I've composed one with the letters B A C H disguised within. Let's see who is clever and discovers it.

FREIDE
On the way back I ran into Krebs. He told me the council's already replaced you with...

SEBASTIAN
Don't tell me. Not now. What does it matter? Friede, give me a light.
    (FRIEDE goes to get a light for SEBASTIAN's pipe)
Why is it so warm in here?
    (Knock at the door. FRIEDE answers it. DR. TAYLOR enters in a black cape, and is rather loud and flamboyant. He carries an official looking bag, which contains primitive instruments, which he will remove during the time he is there. SEBASTIAN quickly puts his pipe away upon hearing his voice)

DR. TAYLOR
Good afternoon, Friede. Anna. Herr Bach, there you are. Well, today we see, yes?

SEBASTIAN
That is the prayer, is it not?

DR. TAYLOR
I am not a praying man, Herr Bach. But I do covet a good attitude in my patients.
    (SEBASTIAN immediately starts coughing again. ANNA looks at Dr. TAYLOR questioningly. He just smiles at her, opens his bag and takes things out)

DR. TAYLOR (Cont'd)
Once these are off and you have your sight again, you will be up and about. Fresh air and movement will help to cure these other ills in your lungs. Now, let's begin.

SEBASTIAN
Friede. Play the composition I have sitting on the harpsichord. I want the good doctor to be inspired while he works.

>   (FREIDE sits at harpsichord and plays the Art of Fugue, Contrapunctus 4, as SEBASTIAN played it before, while bandages are being removed. He unwraps each layer slowly, using an instrument to lift and pull. As he gets to the last layer, he stops momentarily)

DR. TAYLOR
This is the last layer. When I remove it, you may only see us as shadows, until your eyes adjust. But then, shortly, you should see clearly. Are you ready?
>   (SEBASTIAN nods. DR. TAYLOR unwraps the last bandages. FRIDE stops playing)

Now open your eyes.
>   (SEBASTIAN opens his eyes and blinks a few times. He then holds his hand in front of his face. He slowly lowers his hand)

SEBASTIAN
I see nothing. It is total darkness. It's worse than after the first operation.

DR. TAYLOR
I'm sorry. I'm afraid I can do no more today. Let's wait until tomorrow. It may yet improve.
>   (to ANNA, while packing his instruments)

Put cool, moist cloths on the eyes through the night. I will visit tomorrow.
>   (DR. TAYLOR pats SEBASTIAN's arm, exits. ANNA is devastated, and sits at SEBSTIAN's feet. FRIEDE watches, standing off, trying to hide his emotions)

ANNA
My darling. My love. We'll help you. You're not alone. We'll be your eyes.

(ANNA lays her head in his lap, taking his hand in hers)

SEBASTIAN

I was wrong. I **do** see.
    (ANNA is puzzled. FRIEDE is confused and in emotional pain)
Oh, no, not with *these* eyes. I've grown new ones inside. And the wonders they see! It's as you describe in your poems. The love. It's more real than anything on this earth. The light is more penetrating. Great horizons are before me. Hard, and yet soft light. Full of contradictions, yet making perfect sense. It's all so clear. God is pleased.
    (points to harpsichord)
I will have all eternity to finish that work and many more. All eternity.

FREIDE

Father. Forgive me, I...I just want to say I...

SEBASTIAN

Friede! Play the Goldberg, the second aria. I know you know it. It's one of your favorites. Please. Play it for me.

(FRIEDE wants to speak, but ANNA motions for him to play. He sits at the harpsichord and plays Goldberg Variations BWV 988 (Aria II) – Glenn Gould. While FRIEDE plays, ANNA stands and moves to another area, where she takes out her poetry book, and holds it close to her. SEBASTIAN is listening and is moved, but then he stops, thinks, takes off his shoes and throws it at him. FRIEDE stops, suddenly, alarmed, about to protest. SEBASTIAN puts out his arms for FRIEDE to come to him. FRIEDE understands, and goes to him and they embrace. Lights start to go down low on them. ANNA, having watched this, turns and moves downstage. Lights continue to fade slowly behind her, and then on her, as FREIDE continues to play, and she reads her poem, "Rising Like the Morning.")

ANNA

"rising like the morning is your face before me.
gentle lips speaking, without moving.
quiet deep eyes that watch, without judging.
my heart sings at the sight.
you are cool, fragrant, gentle rain on my weary soul.

                    ANNA (Cont'd)
the light of your hands touching my face, is as golden as dawn sun, and evening breeze.
you are a watered garden, heavy with dew and glistening.
my heart beholds you as a feast.
I eat and drink, and am more than satisfied.
I cry for joy...for love of you."

END OF PLAY

As house light go up and audience is leaving:
Play Bach – "Gloria" – Mass in B minor.

for more information

contact

karenklami@gmail.com

www.ingramcontent.com/pod-product-compliance
Lightning Source LLC
Chambersburg PA
CBHW071424160426
43195CB00013B/1804